Out of Joint and the Octagon Theatre, Bolton present

MIXED UP NORTH

by ROBIN SOANS

First performance 10 September 2009
at the Octagon Theatre, Bolton

out of joint

"You expect something special from Out of Joint"
The Times

Out of Joint is a national and international touring theatre company dedicated to the development and production of new writing. Under the direction of Max Stafford-Clark the company has premiered plays from leading writers including David Hare, Caryl Churchill, David Edgar, Alistair Beaton, Sebastian Barry and Timberlake Wertenbaker, as well as introducing first-time writers such as Simon Bennett, Stella Feehily and Mark Ravenhill.

"Max Stafford-Clark's excellent Out of Joint company"
The Independent

Touring all over the UK, Out of Joint frequently performs at and co-produces with key venues such as the Royal Court and the National Theatre and recently with Sydney Theatre Company. The company has performed in six continents. Back home, Out of Joint also pursues an extensive education programme.

"Out of Joint is out of this world"
Boston Globe

Out of Joint's other productions for 2009/10 include *Dreams of Violence* by Stella Feehily (with Soho Theatre) which tours Autumn 2009, and *Andersen's English* by Sebastian Barry in early 2010.

Above: from the Out of Joint productions *Dreams of Violence* (top) and *Talking to Terrorists* (bottom). (Photographs by John Haynes.)

Supported by
**ARTS COUNCIL
ENGLAND**

octagon
Bolton

'The Octagon has been putting the joie de vivre into Bolton for 40 years"
The Guardian

The Octagon Theatre Bolton is a unique producing theatre with a Main Auditorium, built in 1967, featuring a ground-breaking design, with flexible seating offering four separate stage layouts, from thrust to end on. The Octagon produces eight or nine productions annually – including contemporary drama, classics, musical theatre and new plays.

We also co-produce with a number of illustrious partners including Out of Joint, Bush Theatre, Nottingham Playhouse, Northern Broadsides, Hampstead Theatre, York Theatre Royal, Pilot Theatre, Live Theatre and Nitro. In addition, in the last nine years, nine co-productions have toured nationally and beyond including *Blonde Bombshells of 1943*, *The Wedding Dance*, *Lisa's Sex Strike*, *Beautiful Thing*, *East is East* and *Rat Pack Confidential* (with Nottingham Playhouse), which transferred to the West End.

The Octagon has been one of the most garlanded theatres at the prestigious Manchester Evening News Theatre Awards over the last six years, winning sixteen major awards. The Theatre has also received the coveted 'Best Production' award two years in succession – for *Beauty Queen of Leenane* in 2005 and *Blonde Bombshells of 1943* in 2006.

The Octagon recently completed an unprecedentedly successful 40th anniversary season, with the largest and longest programme of plays in its history including five world premieres. The anniversary year exceeded all expectations with audiences rising by thirty percent and generating record ticket sales.

This co-production with Out of Joint is part of our policy of co-producing with creative, imaginative theatre companies of proven excellence to provide our audiences with the highest quality of produced plays to rival any theatre in the country.

We look forward to further collaborations with our colleagues and friends at Out of Joint.

Executive Director: John Blackmore
Artistic Director: David Thacker

The Octagon Theatre
Howell Croft South
Bolton
BL1 1SB

Ticket Office: 01204 520661
General Enquiries: 01204 529407
www.octagonbolton.co.uk

Opposite page: *Road* (above),
Meet the Mukherjees (below).
Above: *Lisa's Sex Strike*

Registered Charity Number 248833

MIXED UP NORTH TOUR 2009

OCTAGON THEATRE BOLTON
10 - 26 Sep
01204 520661 | www.octagonbolton.co.uk

ROYAL & DERNGATE, NORTHAMPTON
29 Sep - 3 Oct
01604 624811 | www.royalandderngate.co.uk

CURVE, LEICESTER
6 - 10 Oct
0116 242 3595 | www.curveonline.co.uk

NUFFIELD THEATRE, SOUTHAMPTON
13 - 17 Oct
023 8067 1771 | www.nuffieldtheatre.co.uk

STONYHURST COLLEGE, CLITHEROE*
19 Oct
www.stonyhurst.ac.uk

BOLTON LADS AND GIRLS CLUB*
20 Oct
www.boltonladsandgirlsclub.co.uk

BOLTON 6TH FORM COLLEGE*
21 Oct
www.bolton-sfc.ac.uk

TURTON HIGH SCHOOL*
22 Oct
www.tmac.uk.com

ACE CENTRE, NELSON*
23 Oct
01282 661080 | www.acecentre.co.uk

DUKES, LANCASTER
28 - 31 Oct
01524 598500 | www.dukes-lancaster.org

LIVERPOOL EVERYMAN
3 - 7 Nov
0151 709 4776 | www.everymanplayhouse.com

WILTON'S MUSIC HALL, LONDON**
10 Nov - 5 Dec
Tickets available from the National Theatre:
020 7452 3000 | www.nationaltheatre.org.uk

*We are very grateful to Clydesdale Bank and Yorkshire Bank; The Granada Foundation; and Unity Theatre Trust for supporting these performances of *Mixed Up North* in community venues in the Burnley area.

**Heartfelt thanks to Sarah Chambers, Sarah Hunt, Michael Straughan and Andrew Wightman at the National Theatre for their time and expertise.

THE COMPANY

In approximate order of appearance

Sarfraz	Kashif Khan
Aftab	Asif Khan
Colin	Matthew Wait
Bella	Kathryn O'Reilly
Tamsin	Lorna Stuart
Trish	Celia Imrie (at certain performances)
	Judith Amsenga (at certain performances)
Jen	Mia Soteriou
Javed	Tyrone Lopez
Kylie	Lisa Kerr
Maureen	Claire Rafferty
Uday	Muzz Khan
Aneesa	Stephanie Street
Wendy	Rose Leslie
Roy	Matthew Wait
Bilal	Tyrone Lopez
Catherine	Claire Rafferty

Director	Max Stafford-Clark
Set Designer	Jonathan Fensom
Lighting Designer	Tim Bray
Sound Designer	Andy Smith
Composer	Felix Cross
Associate Director / Choreographer	Jessica Swale
Costume Supervisor	Fizz Jones
Assistant Director	Elizabeth Newman

Production Manager	Lesley Chenery
Tour Production Manager	Gary Beestone *for Giraffe*
Company and Stage Manager	Helen Keast (Bolton)
Deputy Stage Manager	Sally McKenna (Bolton)
Assistant Stage Manager	Danni Fearnley (Bolton)

JUDITH AMSENGA Trish

Judith Amsenga trained at LAMDA. Credits whilst training include the original production of *Mixed Up North*, *The Cherry Orchard*, *What the Butler Saw* and *The Late Mattia Pascale* (also performed in Bologna). Judith is making her professional stage debut in *Mixed Up North*.

CELIA IMRIE Trish

Celia's theatre credits include *Plague Over England*, *Unsuspecting Susan*, *The Way of the World*, *The Sea* (for which she won the Clarence Derwent Award at the National Theatre), *Seduced* and *Acorn Antiques – The Musical* for which she won an Olivier Award.

Film credits include *St Trinian's, Imagine Me and You*, *Nanny McPhee*, *Wimbledon*, *Calendar Girls*, *Heartland*, *Thunderpants*, *The Borrowers*, *Revelation*, *Lucky Break*, *Bridget Jones's Diary*, *The House of Whipcord* and the *Woody Allen 2009 Summer Project*. Television credits include *After You've Gone*, *Victoria Wood as Seen on TV*, *Pat and Margaret*, *The Commander*, *Kingdom*, *The Lavender List*, *Mr Harvey Lights a Candle*, *Oranges Are Not The Only Fruit*, *The Riff Raff Element*, *A Dark Adapted Eye* and recently filmed *Cranford*.

LISA KERR Kylie

Lisa graduated from LAMDA in 2008. Theatre credits include *The Old 100th* (Rehearsed reading

of Conor Mitchell and Rachel O'Riordan's new writing,Theatre Royal, Drury Lane); *Election Idol* (Puddle Productions, Brighton Fringe Festival); *Peter Pan Kensington Gardens* (Script and Aerial Workshops with Ben Harrison, LAMDA/The Hangar); *The Musician* (Conor Mitchell's new Opera, Old Museum Arts Centre, Belfast); *The Sweetest Swing in Baseball* (LAMDA); *Cole Porter's 'Can-Can'* (LAMDA); *Prince of Tyre* (LAMDA); and *What The Butler Saw* (LAMDA). Film credits include *Re-Uniting the Rubins* and *Klink Klank Echoes*.

ASIF KHAN Aftab

Asif graduated from RADA this year. Theatre credits there include *The Last Days of Judas Iscariot*, *Rookery Nook* (William Gaskill), *Poppy*, *Three Sisters* (Jonathan Miller), *Boxergirl*, *The Pride of Parnell Street*, *The Changeling*, *Antigone*, *Edmond*, *Julius Caesar*, and *The Glass Menagerie*. Theatre prior to training includes *Raining Old Women and Sticks* (North West Stage), *Mulgrave* (Wilson & Wilson), *In God We Trust* (Peshkar Productions), *Silent Cry* (Red Ladder) and *Street Voices* (West Yorkshire Playhouse). Television: Asif is playing Sane Alex in Terry Pratchett's *Going Postal*, which will be screened on Sky One next year. Other film and TV includes *Dalziel and Pascoe*, *Tom*, *Bradford Riots* and *Coronation Street*.

KASHIF KHAN Sarfraz

Kashif graduated from LAMDA in 2009. Theatre credits include *Streets of Rage* (West Yorkshire Playhouse/Tour); *Freeworld* (Contact Theatre/Tour); *Silent Cry* (Lyric Hammersmith/Tour); *Teeth &*

Smiles, Don Juan, Tis Pity She's a Whore, Oedipus Tyrannos, Electra, As You Like It, Comedians, The Man of Mode, The Grace of Mary Traverse, Three Sisters, The Comedy of Errors, The Revenger's Tragedy, Nina, Love you too, Food, The White Devil and *Tommy* (The Musical).

MUZZ KHAN
Uday

Muzz hails from, and spent most of his childhood near, Burnley in Lancashire. He moved to London in 2001 to train as an actor at Webber Douglas. At first, he found London to be quite daunting – having come from a town filled mainly with fields, kebab shops and, at best, a Woolworths! Even *that's* gone now! Since graduating, his theatre credits include *Bully Richard* (Tara Arts); *Fewer Emergencies* (Albany Theatre); *One, Nineteen* (Arcola Theatre); *Blue Funk* (Old Red Lion) and *Felt Effects* (Theatre 503). Television includes *Bradford Riots, No Angels* and *Hetty Wainthropp Investigates*. Films include *Iyi Seneler* and *East Is East*. Radio credits include *Maps For Lost Lovers* and *Street and Lane* for Radio 4. Muzz is also an accomplished DJ and holds a residency at the Pacha nightclub in London.

ROSE LESLIE
Wendy

Rose graduated from the Three Year Acting course at the LAMDA in 2008. She has enjoyed several television and theatre experiences since and has recently won the Scottish BAFTA for Best New Talent, for her performance in the BBC pilot *New Town*. Rose has also enjoyed shooting out on location in Miami and South America for a drama documentary for Channel 5.

Theatre includes touring the country with the Northumberland Theatre Company, playing the young character of Molly in Ann Coburn's production of *Get Up and Tie Your Fingers*.

Other theatre credits whilst training include *Pericles, Caucasian Chalk Circle, Uncle Vanya, Romeo and Juliet, The Country Wife* and *Can-Can*.

TYRONE LOPEZ
Javed/Bilal

Tyrone graduated from London Academy of Music and Dramatic Art 2008. Theatre whilst training includes *Romeo and Juliet, Pericles, Can Can, What the Butler Saw, Uncle Vanya, Not Quite Jerusalem, The Changeling*. Professional theatre credits include, *Amazonia* (a new play by Colin Teevan at the Young Vic Theatre) and *Romeo and Juliet*. Television includes *Caerdydd* where he played the part of Jose in a Welsh Bafta award-winning drama series earlier this year. Film: Tyrone recently finished filming the lead role in *RU486* due for release in May 2010.

KATHRYN
O'REILLY Bella

Kathryn trained at LAMDA and graduated in 2008. This is Kathryn's professional theatrical debut. Prior to training Kathryn played Jocasta in *Oedipus* directed by Marcello Magni and Raquel in *Don Juan* directed by Phil Willmott. Television and film credits include *The Bill, Rough Justice, Halal Harry* and *Zebra Crossings*.

CLAIRE RAFFERTY
Maureen/ Catherine

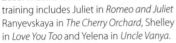

Claire graduated from LAMDA in 2008. Theatre while training includes Juliet in *Romeo and Juliet* Ranyevskaya in *The Cherry Orchard*, Shelley in *Love You Too* and Yelena in *Uncle Vanya*.

Professional credits include *Transition* (Ransom Productions, OMAC Belfast); Huld in *The Trial* (Lyric Theatre Belfast).Television includes *Give My Head Peace* (BBC). Claire recently has been workshopping an Out of Joint and National Theatre co-production about the National Health Service written by Stella Feehily.

MIA SOTERIOU
Jen

Theatre credits include *Turandot* (Hampstead); *Frozen* (Manchester Library); *The Odyssey* (Lyric Hammersmith); *Henry IV 1 and 2* (Bristol Old Vic); *Twelfth Night, Broken Glass* (West Yorks Playhouse); *The Weather, The Arbor, Sgt Ola* (Royal Court); *Comic Mysteries* (Oxford Stage Co/Greenwich); *School for Wives* (ETT); *The Government Inspector, Cyrano De Bergerac* (Greenwich); *Spring Awakening* (Sheffield Crucible); *Lennon* (West End/Liverpool); *Stags and Hens* (Liverpool); *Arabian Nights, The Merchant of Venice* (Shared Experience); *Bed of Roses* (Hull Truck). Television credits include *The Bill, Holby City, Like Father Like Son, EastEnders, TLC, Merseybeat, Kid in the Corner, Sunburn, Peak Practice, Where the Heart Is, Casualty, Absolutely Fabulous, Brookside, Murder Most Horrid, Alas Smith and Jones,* and *The Chief.*

Films include *Mamma Mia!, Eastern Promises, Topsy Turvy,* and *Secrets and Lies.*

Mia also composes for theatre, TV and radio.

STEPHANIE STREET Aneesa

Stephanie trained at LAMDA and studied English at Cambridge University. Theatre credits include *The Contingency Plan* (The Bush); *Shades* (Royal Court); *Sweet Cider* (Arcola); *Not the End of the World* (Bristol Old Vic); *Too Close to Home* (Lyric); *The Laramie Project* (Kit Productions); *The Vagina Monologues* (UK tour); *Dark Meaning Mouse* (Finborough); *As You Like It* (Greenwich Observatory); *Much Ado About Nothing* (Lamb Players), and *Arabian Nights* (ATC). Television credits include *Monday Monday, Apparitions, Holby City, Never Better, EastEnders, Primeval, Commander III, Soundproof, Coming Up 2005 – Heavenly Father, Nylon, Twenty Things to Do Before You're Thirty, Red Cap* and *The Last Detective.* Stephanie is a Selector for the National Student Drama Festival. As a writer her first play, *Sisters,* is going on at Sheffield Crucible in 2010.

LORNA STUART
Tamsin

Lorna trained at LAMDA. Theatre credits include Susan in *The Lion, the Witch and the Wardrobe* (Antic Disposition) and Beakie in *Honk!* (Hotbox). Theatre whist training include Grusha in *The Caucasian Chalk Circle*, Thaisa in *Pericles*, Eve in *Can Can* and Varya in *The Cherry Orchard.* Television credits include Jen in *AAA* (Endemol). Voice Overs include *Poetry of Abandonment.*

Lorna played Tamsin in *Mixed Up North* at LAMDA.

MATTHEW WAIT
Colin/Roy

Theatre includes
Erpingham Camp
(Brighton Festival);
Piranha Heights (Soho
Theatre); *Rita Sue and
Bob Too, A State Affair,
Some Explicit Polaroids* (Out of Joint); *Cool
Water Murder* (Belgrade Theatre); *Down
Red Lane, Rough* (Birmingham Rep); *Certain
Young Men* (Almeida); *Tartuffe, Birdy* (PW
Productions); *Pitchfork Disney, The Marowitz
Hamlet* (Citizens Theatre Glasgow); *Bad
Company, Weldon Rising* (Royal Court).
Television includes *Heartbeat, Coronation
Street, The Bill, Silent Witness, Casualty,
Heroes and Villains, Inspector Lynley, Holby
City, Submerged, Wing and a Prayer, Where
the Heart Is, Out of the Blue, Crocodile Shoes,
99:1, Peak Practice, Pie in the Sky, Young
Indiana Jones Chronicles, Sam Saturday*
and *Clarissa*.

TIM BRAY
Lighting Designer

Tim is pleased to return to Out of Joint
and work with Max again. Tim's Lighting
Design credits include *The Rover, Iphigenia*
(Southwark Playhouse); *Sisters Such
Devoted Sisters* (Drill Hall), *Macbeth* (The
Albany, Deptford); *Machinal* (BAC); *Out
Of The Blue* (Nottingham Playhouse);
One Day In October (Riverside Studios);
Sara (The Bridewell); and *Jamais Vu* (Ken
Cambell). Tim has toured extensively
re-lighting various productions including:
Sweeney Todd (RNT); *Anna Karenina*
(Shared Experience); *Oliver Twist* (Lyric
Hammersmith); *A Midsummer Night's
Dream* (Tim Supple); *Convict's Opera, The
Overwhelming* (National Theatre/Out of
Joint): *O Go My Man* (Out of Joint/Royal
Court), *Top Girls* (Oxford Stage Company);
The 39 Steps (Fiery Angel); *The Glass
Menagerie* (Theatre Royal Bath); *The Dumb
Waiter* (Oxford Playhouse); *Highland Fling*
(Matthew Bourne) and *Fat Pig* (Comedy
Theatre).

GRAHAM COWLEY
Producer

Out of Joint's Producer since 1998. His
long collaboration with Max Stafford-Clark
began as Joint Stock Theatre Group's first
General Manager for seven years in the
1970s. He was General Manager of the
Royal Court for eight years, and on their
behalf transferred a string of hit plays to
the West End. His career has spanned the
full range of theatre production, from
small fringe companies to major West End
shows and large scale commercial tours.
Outside Out of Joint, he has translated
Véronique Olmi's *End of Story* (Chelsea
Theatre) and has produced the 'Forgotten
Voices from the Great War' series of plays
including *What the Women Did* (Southwark
Playhouse, 2004), *Red Night* by James
Lansdale Hodson (Finborough, 2005)

and *My Real War 1914-?*, based on the letters of a young WW1 soldier, which toured twice in 2007 and runs at Trafalgar Studios in October 2009. The final play in the series, *The Searcher* by Velona Pilcher, is due to appear at Wilton's Music Hall in January 2010.

FELIX CROSS
Composer

Felix has been Nitro's Artistic Director since 1996. For Nitro his credits include *The Wedding Dance* (writer and co-directer); *Mass Carib* (composer, director); *The Evocation of Papa Mas* (composer, lyricist); *High Heeled Parrotfish* (MD); *Slamdunk* (writer, co-director); *Passports to the Promised Land* (writer, composer); *Tricksters' Payback* (composer and lyricist); *ICED* (director); *An African Cargo* (director); *An Evening of Soul Food* (director) and *Up Against The*

Wall (co-writer). He has also written the musicals *Blues for Railton* (Albany Empire) and *Glory!* (Temba) and composed the music for over seventy stage, TV and radio productions including *Macbeth*, *Talking to Terrorists*, *O Go My Man*, *The Overwhelming*, *Convicts Opera* (Out of Joint); *Ghostdancing*, *Ryman and The Sheik*, *Strictly Dandia*, *A Fine Balance*, *Wuthering Heights* (Tamasha); *The Bottle Imp* and *Jekyll and Hyde* (Major Road).

JONATHAN FENSOM
Designer

Jonathan was nominated for a Tony Award for his Broadway set design of *Journey's End* in 2007 the production also won the Tony Award for Best Revival. Jonathan was Associate Designer on

Disney's *The Lion King*, which premiered at the New Amsterdam Theatre on Broadway and has subsequently opened

worldwide. He has designed more than 50 productions worldwide, from

Shakespeare, Ballet and modern classics. Some of his recent productions include *King Lear, Love's Labours Lost* (Shakespeare's Globe); *Swan Lake* (San Francisco Ballet); *The Faith Healer, Journey's End, The American Plan, Pygmalion* (New York); *Rain Man, Blackbird, Crown Matrimonial, Some Girls, Twelfth Night* (West End); *The Homecoming, Big White Fog* (Almeida Theatre); *Happy Now?, The Mentalists, Burn/Citizenship/Chatroom* (National Theatre); *Talking to Terrorists* (Out of Joint/Royal Court); *The Sugar Syndrome* (Royal Court); *National Anthems* (Old Vic).

ROBIN SOANS
Writer

Recent work as an actor includes *On the Beach* and *Resilience* at the Bush Theatre, *Midsomer Murders* for television, and his latest two film appearances have been in *Pierrepoint* and *The Queen*. As a writer: *Bet Noir* (Young Vic studio); *Sinners and Saints* (Croydon Warehouse); *A State Affair* (Out-of-Joint tour and Soho, and Radio 3); *The Arab Israeli Cookbook* (Gate Theatre and Tricycle, Los Angeles and Tokyo, and B.B.C. World Service); *Talking to Terrorists* (Out of Joint and Royal Court, Dublin, Toronto and Tokyo and Radio 3) and *Life After Scandal* (Hampstead Theatre and Radio 4).

ANDY SMITH
Sound Designer

Andy was born and bred in Bolton. After moving away and completing a degree in contemporary theatre at Lancaster University he briefly worked as a technician for a production company in Oxford before returning home to Bolton. Since starting at the Octagon eight years ago Andy has progressed to become Chief Electrician and still loves designing the sound for Octagon productions. Andy has been nominated as part of Best Design teams on numerous occasions at the MEN Theatre Awards and was a member of the team that won the award for the Octagon production of *Oh What a Lovely War!* in 2008 *Beautiful Thing* in 2005.

MAX STAFFORD-CLARK
Director

Educated at Trinity College, Dublin, Max Stafford-Clark co-founded Joint Stock Theatre Group in 1974 following his Artistic Directorship of The Traverse Theatre, Edinburgh. From 1979 to 1993 he was Artistic Director of The Royal Court Theatre. In 1993 he founded the touring company, Out of Joint. His work as a Director has overwhelmingly been with new writing, and he has commissioned and directed first productions by many leading writers, including Sue Townsend, Stephen Jeffreys, Timberlake Wertenbaker, Sebastian Barry, April de Angelis, Mark Ravenhill, Andrea Dunbar, Robin Soans, Alistair Beaton, Stella Feehily, David Hare and Caryl Churchill. In addition he has directed classic texts including *The Seagull*, *The Recruiting Officer* and *King Lear* for the Royal Court; *A Jovial Crew*, *The Wives' Excuse* and *The Country Wife* for The Royal Shakespeare Company; and *The Man of Mode*, *She Stoops to Conquer*, *Three Sisters* and *Macbeth* for Out of Joint. He directed David Hare's *The Breath of Life* for Sydney Theatre Company in 2003, and *The Overwhelming* at the Roundabout Theatre, New York, in 2007. Academic credits include an honorary doctorate from Oxford Brookes University and Visiting Professorships at the Universities of Hertfordshire, Warwick and York. His books are *Letters to George* and *Taking Stock*. Most recently he recently directed *Dreams of Violence* for Out of Joint and Soho Theatre (currently touring).

JESSICA SWALE
Associate Director/ Choreographer

Jessica is resident Associate Director at Out of Joint, having also worked on *Dreams of Violence* (with Soho Theatre, touring Autumn 09), and as Assistant Director on *The Overwhelming* (National Theatre and tour). Recent credits include, as Artistic Director of Red Handed Theatre Company: *The School for Scandal*, *A Midsummer Night's Dream*, *Twelfth Night* (Bridewell Theatre); *The Glass Tower* (Pleasance Theatre); *Finding Alice* (Edinburgh and Luton); *Lost Luggage* (Theatre Royal Haymarket); *Bare* and *Baghdad Baby* (Camden People's Theatre). As movement director: *Red Fortress* (Unicorn Theatre); *Medeia* (Union Theatre); *Queer Bent for the Tudor Gent* (American Globe, New York); and *A Starry Night* at Salisbury Cathedral – her first experience of directing a camel (rather a diva). Jessica is an associate director for Youth Bridge Global, an International NGO which uses theatre in war torn or disadvantaged countries. As such she directed *A Comedy of Errors* in the Marshall Islands in 2008 and traveled to Bosnia this Summer to work on *Much Ado about Nothing*. Jessica is also the author of *Drama Games: For Workshops Classrooms and Rehearsals*. Her new book, *Drama Games: For Devising*, is to be published by Nick Hern Books in early 2009. Jessica's first play *Mad Kings and Englishmen* plays at the Bridewell Theatre from October.

MIXED UP NORTH

First published in 2009 by Oberon Books Ltd
521 Caledonian Road, London N7 9RH
Tel: 020 7607 3637 / Fax: 020 7607 3629
e-mail: info@oberonbooks.com
www.oberonbooks.com

A catalogue record for this book is available from the British
Library.

ISBN: 978-1-84002-960-4

Cover design by Jon Bradfield, from photographs by
Joel Chester Fildes and William Chitham

Printed in Great Britain by CPI Antony Rowe, Chippenham.

ACKNOWLEDGEMENTS

This play was researched in Burnley during 2007 and 2008.

Special thanks to Jesse Quinones for his help and advice in the research. The play was developed through The Long Project at LAMDA 2007, so thanks to Peter James, Phil Ormrod, and the students; and to Max Stafford-Clark, who directed the first workshop; and to Max, Graham Cowley and Out of Joint for financing the later stages of research.

And thanks to all the contributors in Burnley, who gave up a great deal of time to make us welcome.

Characters

TRISH (57)
a senior youth worker

BELLA (30)
a director in young people's community theatre

TAMSIN (22)
a trainee youth worker, and an assistant director
and actor in community theatre

JEN (52)
a community worker

COLIN (34)
a politically incorrect youth worker, and
a technician in community theatre

UDAY (22)
a trainee youth worker and assistant to Trish

ANEESA (32)
a trainee youth worker and part-time assistant
to Trish

SARFRAZ (20)
an assistant stage manager in community theatre

AFTAB (20)
an actor in community theatre

JAVED (18)
an actor in community theatre

MAUREEN (18)
Javed's ambitious girlfriend

KYLIE (16)
an actor in community theatre

WENDY (16)
an actor in community theatre

CATHERINE (28)
an Irish community facilitator married to...

BILAL (27)
a community facilitator

ROY (55)
a County Officer

The parts of JAVED and MAUREEN should be doubled with
CATHERINE and BILAL.
The part of COLIN should be doubled with ROY.

/ means the next actor should start speaking at that point.

Act One

A youth group is getting ready for the dress rehearsal of their play in the main hall of a community centre on the edge of Burnley. Music plays... Pet Shop Boys' version of 'You Were Always on my Mind'.

Mid-stage is the set for the Rikki Rajah Show.

There is a table behind the set, where food is being assembled.

The back wall is full of posters, graffiti, and has a basketball net in the middle. Table football to the side. SARFRAZ and AFTAB are playing Fußball.

COLIN is at work at the lighting panel behind the audience.

BELLA has a clipboard, and is comparing notes with TAMSIN. The director's table is to the side of the set. BELLA is seven months pregnant.

JEN is in the kitchen offstage.

There is a dressing room and costume area at the back. COLIN goes up to the control panel and turns off the music.

COLIN: OK, Sarfraz...

SARFRAZ: Yeah?

COLIN: Kill the workers.

SARFRAZ flicks a switch and all the lights on stage go out.

BELLA: NO, Colin NO! I'm still working!

COLIN: Alright Bella. Sorry. Sorry Sarfraz.

The lights come back on.

BELLA: Thank you.

TRISH comes on. She notices a group of five people sitting in the middle of the audience.

TRISH: Oh you're here then...that's good. Bella told me she
had some guests coming, and you were interested in 'Street

YY' and the work we do sort of thing, but to be honest with you, what with one thing and another, it had quite slipped mi mind. So…anyway… I'm Trish, and it's very nice to see you here, and who would like a brew? It'll be half an hour before we start…

COLIN: You'll be lucky…

TRISH: About half an hour…can I get you a brew in the meanwhile? The cakes are on their way, they'll be here in a minute…all home made…very nice. You could manage a slice of cake I'm sure.

JEN hurries past with a plate of butties.

JEN: They should have been here an hour ago.

TRISH: Well give Len a ring. I've got people waiting.

TRISH goes to the kitchen.

COLIN: He's picking up a speaker as well.

JEN: Right.

JAVED saunters out of the dressing room. He sees the visitors in the audience.

JAVED: Who are they?

BELLA: Just some friends of mine. They've come to watch the dress rehearsal. Don't worry…they'll be supportive. And if you've got something interesting to say about the work, they'd like to know.

JEN hurries off as KYLIE comes from the dressing room. KYLIE is on the phone.

KYLIE: No, Rio, it's over.

She sees the visitors, and looks at JAVED.

JAVED: Friends of Bella's. If you've got something interesting to say about the work, they'd like to know.

KYLIE: Like Wendy being a lezzer.

BELLA: Kylie.

22

JAVED lies back in an armchair. MAUREEN comes on, and snuggles up to him. They snog.

KYLIE: No, Rio. We aren't even going out any more. Over means over means over. Right? (*Switches off phone.*)

BELLA: Pack it in. Javed, you've got lines to learn.

MAUREEN: You're only jealous.

MAUREEN starts to go off almost colliding with JEN coming on with a bowl of salad.

JEN: Mind yerself.

MAUREEN: No-one's gonna eat that.

MAUREEN goes. JAVED picks up a basket ball. UDAY and ANEESA come on with a folded sheet of paper, which they give to BELLA.

UDAY: It's the programme…do you want to look it over?

BELLA: Brilliant…thanks. Tamsin?

TAMSIN: Yeah.

BELLA: Check it, will you? Just make sure we've not missed anybody off.

TAMSIN: Right.

JEN: (*To UDAY and ANEESA as she goes.*) Give us a hand.

JEN, UDAY and ANEESA go into the kitchen as TRISH re-enters with a cup of tea.

JAVED throws the ball into the basketball net.

TRISH: No, Javed, absolutely not. You know the rules. No basketball.

JAVED leans against the Fußball table. AFTAB still playing Fußball.

SARFRAZ tries to adjust a lamp on a stand with a long pole.

SARFRAZ: Motherfucker.

WENDY comes out of the dressing room area. She looks slightly alarmed at the sight of the visitors. She searches the set. She has a bandage on the back of her neck.

WENDY: Has anyone seen mi bag?

KYLIE starts flirting with JAVED. MAUREEN comes back on and sees.

KYLIE: (*Squeaky voice.*) Has anyone seen mi bag?

MAUREEN: Don't you dare, you slapper.

BELLA: Maureen! Out! Javed, lines. Now!

MAUREEN goes. JAVED goes into the dressing room. TRISH perches for a second, and talks to the visitors in the audience.

TRISH: Are you not like me…grabbing a moment's peace in the middle of mayhem? It does something for the equil… what's that word? Is it equilibrium? Oh you'll get me using long words, putting me in front of a few theatre people. Oh I'm just me really…you'll get used to me. What you looking for Wendy?

WENDY: I've lost mi bag…mi make-up bag.

COLIN: I put it there, Wendy.

TRISH: Colin!

COLIN: Alright!

COLIN throws the bag to WENDY. She goes and sits quietly on the arm of the armchair.

UDAY and ANEESA bring on two bowls of crisps each. The empty packets are on top. JEN follows them to the table, takes the empty packets and puts them by the side of each bowl.

UDAY and ANEESA lay out the paper plates and cups.

TRISH: What did Len say?

JEN: He's not answering his phone.

TRISH: He'll be on his way then.

JEN goes. KYLIE gets another call on her mobile phone.

KYLIE: I don't believe this. No Rio, how many times do I have to tell you? I'm working. This is the third time you've phoned me in ten minutes.

COLIN: (*To SARFRAZ.*) Sarfraz... You'll need the ladder for that.

SARFRAZ goes off.

KYLIE: No, this is sexual harassment. We aren't even going out any more. You do not control me. Fuck off.

BELLA: Kylie, shut up! Colin?

COLIN: Yeah.

BELLA: Can I just scrub the second highlight? On page 33.

COLIN: Scrub it altogether?

BELLA: Let's go straight to the third contestant.

TAMSIN: Straight to the third contestant.

COLIN: It means another lighting change.

TAMSIN: (*To BELLA.*) It means another lighting change.

BELLA: Is that alright?

TAMSIN: Is that alright?

COLIN: Give me a minute.

TAMSIN: Give him a minute.

TRISH: Colin's in charge of light and sound. I'm sure he won't mind me saying but it's a bit of a sad time really, in't it Colin?

COLIN: That's one way of putting it.

TRISH: Bereavement in the family.

COLIN: Mi step-dad...don't worry...we weren't that close...

TRISH: And the funeral's tomorrow. We thought we might have to cancel the show, but Colin says Sarfraz can do it.

COLIN: He's more than capable.

SARFRAZ comes on with a ladder.

TRISH: He's turning out to be a bit of a whiz on the electrics is our Sarfraz.

SARFRAZ: (*Nearly electrocuting himself.*) Motherfucker.

TRISH: But that's 'Street YY' for you. You alright Wendy?

WENDY: I couldn't find mi make-up bag, that's all.

WENDY goes back to the dressing room. UDAY and ANEESA go back to the kitchen.

TRISH: When I wake up in the morning, the first thing I see is the Hameldon Hills to one side, and then I look across to Pendle Hill the other way, and it reminds me of the opening of Psalm 121… 'I will lift up mine eyes unto the hills, from whence cometh my help', and I think the Lord will be on my side and it will be a good day.

JEN hurries on with the last of the food.

JEN: Food's ready.

TRISH: Did you all hear? Food's ready. Aftab?

AFTAB: Yeah?

TRISH: You could stop that a minute. The food's ready.

BELLA: Can you all make sure you're not wearing costumes. We don't want food on the costumes.

TRISH: No eating in costumes. And there's plates…paper plates. Is there anyone left in the dressing room?

WENDY: (*Entering.*) Yes.

TRISH: Anyone else?

WENDY: Javed.

TRISH: You should grab yourself some food. You've not got long you know.

WENDY: Javed. Food.

JAVED joins WENDY and they go to get some food.

BELLA: (*To TAMSIN.*) Go and grab yourself some food. Give yourself a break.

TAMSIN: Shall I bring you something?

BELLA: No, I can't say I fancy anything at the moment.

TAMSIN: Won't be long.

TAMSIN goes to get some food.

TRISH: (*To AFTAB.*) Aftab. That's not yer costume is it?

AFTAB: No.

TRISH: Right. (*To visitors.*) We've done the 'technical rehearsal' and we're about to start the 'dress rehearsal', and they're just grabbing something to eat. A lot of young people here have never acted before. Wendy's not acted before…it's your first play in't it Wendy?

WENDY: Yes.

TRISH: You see…and I think the whole situation with the lights and the set and the costumes and what have you is quite overawing for them…specially now you lot have arrived. (*Shouts.*) Use the plates!

JEN: Egg mayonnaise, tuna, cheese and onion, salad…

TRISH: This is Jen, who runs the Community Centre.

JEN curtsies.

Very nice, very nice…you should try some salad to put on your butties. Aftab, do you want some salad on your buttie?

AFTAB: No.

TRISH: You should try some. It's good for you.

TAMSIN: You didn't ask me about my first driving lesson.

TRISH: We've got other things on our minds. How did it go…your first driving lesson?

TAMSIN: Yeah, it went alright. I didn't kill anyone.

TRISH: Oh good Tamsin, I'm pleased. (*Shouts.*) Use the plates… Kylie, use a plate, please…respect the place. Have you had some salad?

KYLIE: No.

TRISH: Oh dear.

JEN: Crisps over there… I've put the empty packets by each bowl so you can see the different flavours.

JEN hurries off.

TRISH: Wherever I've gone people have either liked me or loathed me, but I've always made a wave. You can't meet me without thinking something about me. I do think I'm a gateway to a lot of things. Right…so…how did I come to be in Burnley? Well… Wendy?

WENDY: Yeah?

TRISH: Is that a bandage? What have you done to your neck?

WENDY: Nothing. I'm fine.

WENDY goes out quickly, leaving her food.

TRISH: You alright Wendy? Wendy? Aftab?

AFTAB: Yeah?

TRISH: Can I have a word? (*Taking him to one side.*)

SARFRAZ: Where do you want it pointing?

COLIN: On the chair.

TRISH: Do you mind my asking…there seems to be something…

AFTAB: Wendy?

TRISH: Yes. She's not her usual self if you don't mind me saying.

AFTAB: She's been like that all weekend.

TRISH: Shall I try and have a word, or is that interfering?

AFTAB: It's nothing to do with us if that's what you're thinking. Well I don't think it is.

TRISH: Right. Thanks for that. (*To visitors.*) Excuse me a minute…

TRISH goes out.

BELLA: Sarfraz, I haven't asked… how did it go this morning?

COLIN: Oh yeah /…how did it go?

AFTAB: How / did it go?

KYLIE: How did it go?

SARFRAZ: Have to go back motherfuckers. I have to go back on mi birthday, 10th October. (*To visitors.*) I was in court today for a fight at McDonalds. These white boys came in, took my mate's milkshake and poured it on him.

AFTAB: What flavour?

SARFRAZ: Strawberry. Fuckers. They died, motherfuckers. I got shit on me, milkshake on me, and after the milkshake they started calling us black-ass motherfuckers. How dick I was, how fucked I was, they said 'Fuck you, you mother son of a black bitch, go back to your own country.' One guy had a knuckle duster, so I took my belt off, wrapped it round my left hand; I got up, I said, 'You're going down bitch…boom bang.' When I fight, I make that sound… 'poom'…that's from six months working as security on club doors, so I'm fit… I went on a course…one-hundred and ninety down I paid for it.

AFTAB: I couldn't do it.

SARFRAZ: You can't do it 'cos you're fat…a big fat Dacca dog. Why are you laughing?

AFTAB: He always makes me laugh.

SARFRAZ: I make you laugh twenty-four seven. The guy I knocked out was on an ASBO.

BELLA: ASBOs. What a ridiculous concept. In Burnley, it's quite cool to have an ASBO.

AFTAB: Might as well have something. Most people have got nothing.

SARFRAZ: Reedly Court…juvenile court. Six of them… magistrate type people…all white…one of them was being a dick… I told him he was a dick. He looked at me over his glasses and said, 'Tut, tut, tut.' So I said 'Tut, tut, tut.' Another guy told me to calm down.

JEN comes in with a plate of Wagon Wheels.

JEN: I found some Wagon Wheels and some Penguins.

COLIN: If you've done that, disconnect the speaker.

SARFRAZ: That one.

COLIN: Yeah…that one.

JEN: No-one's eaten any salad.

BELLA: Can you fix it?

COLIN: No, it's packed up. Len's bringing the spare one.

BELLA: Where is Len?

JEN: He's on his way…at least we hope he is.

JEN exits. JAVED eats a Wagon Wheel.

JAVED: I never get trouble.

AFTAB: / You're wrong.

SARFRAZ: You're wrong. He's wrong.

AFTAB: You get trouble all the time.

SARFRAZ: Walking down the street with Maureen…four or five skinheads behind yer…

AFTAB: With the pitbulls…

SARFRAZ: 'Go on boy…eat…'

JAVED: I've not heard them say that.

AFTAB: You never hear anything.

MAUREEN comes on.

MAUREEN: Javed, can I have a word?

JAVED: Do you want something to eat?

MAUREEN: No, I want a word with you in private.

MAUREEN and JAVED go into the dressing room.

SARFRAZ: There's a lot of shit man.

AFTAB: There's a lot of weirdos…

SARFRAZ: Too many weirdos…

AFTAB: We have old people…they're odd…paedos, rapists, prosi-hunters; we don't have gay people…

BELLA: I have to say Burnley's a very bad town to be gay in. There's only one place…it's called The Garden Bar…it's a haven for misfits…there's two midgets go in there, people with special needs, and a brother and sister who have an incestuous relationship…it's not a great place for a night out.

TRISH hurries back in.

TRISH: What on earth are you talking about?

BELLA: The Garden Bar.

TRISH: They don't want to know about that place…needs looking at. Now did any of you see which way Wendy went?

AFTAB: Have you tried the workshop?

TRISH: That's an idea. And another thing about The Garden Bar…it's the drugs.

TRISH hurries out.

BELLA: It is a good place to score drugs 'cos some of the gay guys do a lot of stuff when they're doing what they're doing, and some of the lads go in there to score Es.

AFTAB: A lot of crack-heads, a lot of pot-heads…

SARFRAZ: A lot of pot-heads…a lot of mother fuckers doing that shit. A lot of joy-riders.

AFTAB: I was champion joy-rider.

SARFRAZ: Motherfucker.

AFTAB: Years of joy-riding… I never got busted by the police. As soon as I got my licence, I got three points. I was on a dual carriageway and there was a police officer in the other lane… I looked at him…he looked at me…he was going, 'What, what, what?' So I started going…

SARFRAZ: / 'What, what, what?'

AFTAB: 'What, what, what?' He put his flash on. I had to pull up. I showed him my documents…they were all OK…he checked the steering wheel, looked under the bonnet… I had a battery holder. The lights were working. He jacked all four tyres up. He had a little measuring thing to measure the tread…

SARFRAZ: It was the tread…he got you on the tread.

AFTAB: All the tyres were alright…he got to the driver's side, there was this little wire hanging down out the grip. He said, 'Ha ha ha mate.' He gave me a sixty pound fine and three points on mi license. We sent him a letter…first class stamp…we wore rubber gloves so they couldn't get fingerprints… 'Motherfucker, die tonight…'

SARFRAZ: 'You're gonna die…gonna die tonight; we're gonna bomb your car…letter bomb through your door…'

AFTAB: 'Al Qaeda's gonna bomb you…'

SARFRAZ: 'The Taliban's gonna bomb you…'

AFTAB: 'The Teletubbies are gonna bomb you…'

SARFRAZ: 'Ipsy, Dipsy, Lala, Po. They're all gonna bomb you motherfucker.'

AFTAB: So after paying the fine and everything…we had this shop, new shop in Flag Street, and he used to park his car outside it. We'd egg it…throw eggs at it, carroted it…

SARFRAZ: Onions, lettuce, potatoes, apples…

AFTAB: But not peppers… I like peppers…popped his tyres and everything, for a week. Got all my friends to do it. What we did…we'd get two litre bottles of Coca-Cola… we'd drink half of it, and then fill it with piss…everyone pisses in it… I was the first one…and then pour it on the car…pour it over the windows, and the door handles…like sticky…every day for a week. We didn't see him after that. I was going to write him a love note.

TRISH comes back in.

TRISH: Not there. She's not come back in has she?

TAMSIN: Haven't seen her.

TRISH: I can't think where she went. Have you had some butties?

SARFRAZ: Not yet.

TRISH: I should get some before they all go.

SARFRAZ gets some food.

Use the plates. There's some paper plates. And try and eat some salad. Tamsin, did you have some salad?

TAMSIN: No thanks.

TRISH: Right. Now then…how I came to be in Burnley was…what happened was…after 'The Disturbances' there was all this government money floating about and the Head of the Church in Burnley rang me to say he'd got hold of some of it and he'd tried to use it but it had all gone pear-shaped…wondered if I could help sort it out. I was working in Bolton at the time, so I didn't know about the ethical side of things…but lots of people in Burnley were all saying 'Trish, you should be here…these are extraordinary times…nothing like this has ever happened to the town before…we need some people with a good grounding of professional experience, and we need them fast…you could at least ask your bosses if there's the possibility of a transfer.'

I went away on holiday to Greece…it was good going away 'cos you can look at the problem from a distance… are you following me…and I was praying a lot, and seeking God's Face…when you have a problem, that's what we call it…seeking God's Face, and 'putting a fleece before him'…

MAUREEN comes in and sits down in the auditorium.

Hello Maureen, can I help you?

MAUREEN: I've come to watch.

TRISH: I'm not sure…has Bella said you can?

BELLA: No, I said you couldn't. It's tomorrow you can come. This is private…it's just for the actors.

MAUREEN: Who's this lot?

BELLA: They're my guests…do you mind.

MAUREEN: Javed said I could come.

TRISH: And is it for Javed to say?

BELLA: Tomorrow, tomorrow's the public performance. We've got our work cut out as it is. I don't want any distractions.

MAUREEN: Javed said he doesn't mind.

BELLA: It's not for Javed to say. Where is he?

MAUREEN: He's in the dressing room.

BELLA: Send him to me please and I'll have a word; I'm sorry but this is just for the actors.

MAUREEN goes out.

I'm sorry, but she can't stay…she's sat in half the rehearsals, and she chips in every five minutes, it's a nightmare…sometimes they've snogged all through rehearsals…and he's threatened to leave on a number of occasions, hurling his script across the room, saying he's had enough…but he's always come back the next week.

TRISH: He can be a little bit difficult he can at times, Javed… you know what it's like…but he's very good when he puts his mind to it. He's playing what you might call the lead part, Rikki Rajah.

Anyway, talk about the path of opportunity being opened up for me…when I got back from my holiday, I pressed the message thing on mi phone…it's mi boss in Bolton… 'Could I go to a meeting?'

JEN comes in.

JEN: Anyone want a brew?

TRISH: I'm fine thanks.

COLIN: I could do wi' a brew…two sugars.

JEN: I'll bring you one. Bella?

BELLA: I'm fine thanks Jen. I need to start getting everyone back in by ten past.

JEN: You've not had anything to eat have you. I'm sorry but I'm insisting. You can't go on and on.

TAMSIN: No you can't.

JEN: I've got some Sugar Puffs, what about a bowl of Sugar Puffs?

BELLA: You've not got any Dairylea Spread have you?

JEN: I can do Dairylea Spread. On white?

BELLA: White, no butter. (*To us.*) It's all I'm eating at the moment. It's not lumps of coal or anything like that. (*To JEN.*) You've not got a jar of Piccalilli have you?

JEN: I have.

BELLA: With a bit of piccalilli.

JEN: You see.

BELLA: And a banana.

JEN: Now you're talking. (*Going.*)

COLIN: I'll have a banana if you're offering.

JEN: (*Off.*) Right.

TRISH: I had the meeting, on the way out I said, 'James, can I have a word about something else?' 'Course you can Trish.' I started off the conversation with, 'You know I'm a Christian?' He said, 'Yes.' I said, 'Well I don't know if this makes sense…don't worry about having to knock me back… I'm used to taking knocks in life… I need to ask you something serious. I want to know if there's a possibility of a transfer to Burnley, 'cos I feel I'm needed there.'

He just looked at me and said, 'I'm not a Christian, you know that Trish, but at times like this I think there might be something in it. It just so happens I need someone in Burnley; and it can't just be any old body…it's a difficult job and it needs someone with vision and understanding.' And I said, 'Well you know me, James, I've never not hit mi targets.' The job was to do with the Government Task Force report on 'The Disturbances'…the 2001 Disturbances… Lord Clark had said that the VFCS hadn't been given its rightful voice and place within the life of Burnley really…that's the Voluntary Faith and Community Sector…and he thought the most important work was likely to be done from within the community so to speak.

COLIN: If you work for the Council, you have to call what happened in 2001 'Disturbances'…you're not allowed to call them riots, which is a pile of piss, 'cos to me the best part of eighty hairy-arsed blokes going on a rampage, turning over cars, and setting fire to them, and smashing things up, is a fucking riot. But it weren't a race riot… everyone says about Burnley… 'Oh they had race riots.' That's bollocks. It only started 'cos all these skinheads who were bored out of their fucking brains all got pissed.

JEN: (*Coming back in with a cup of tea.*) It was a scary, scary experience. I phoned my friend in Todmorden... 'Can I come and stay for three days?' There were petrol bombs coming through windows...me and my husband slept downstairs...if a petrol bomb had come through window, it would have landed on the bed.

UDAY and ANEESA come in.

ANEESA: Were you looking for Wendy?

TRISH: Where is she?

UDAY: Out in the car park.

TRISH: Right...these are two of my key workers from the Asian community...this is Uday and this is Aneesa. They've both had time off from 'Street YY' for one reason or another, and I'm sure they'll tell you about it if they want to.

ANEESA: I were getting married that's all, and having a baby. Nothing unusual in that.

TRISH: You did disappear off the radar.

ANEESA: That's because I went to Pakistan.

BELLA: 'Went' being a bit of a euphemism quite frankly.

ANEESA: Bella!

BELLA: Alright, alright.

TRISH: Anyway, they've all got a story. In the car park did you say?

UDAY: Yes.

ANEESA: Yes, she's standing under the trees.

TRISH: Right. I'll have a word before we start.

TRISH leaves.

COLIN: The police...they were like sheep dogs...they pretty much shepherded these Neanderthal hairy-arsed bloody thugs down Colne Road, into the town centre...now as you get into town, you pass a whole row of shops, and all of them were Asian-owned, and this is going to sound stereotypical…but they were nearly all taxi ranks or take-aways… (*JEN gives him the cup of tea.*) …thanks…so what do they do…all these pissed-up blokes…smashed the shops up…

JEN: Which got all the Asians stirred up.

COLIN: Which got all the Asians stirred up.

JEN: They came out of all the houses in Daneshouse and Stoneyholme…like the doors were all opening and they came out in a whole mass of them…like the whole street were packed wi' em…Dairylea Spread. (*Goes.*)

COLIN: Banana.

JEN: (*Off.*) Banana.

COLIN: The Asian angry mob were rioting with police in Duke Bar, and they set fire to the Duke of York pub and completely burned it out.

UDAY: I never saw any Asian on white in the riots in the main part of it…it was Asian on police and white on police.

BELLA: After the riots hit, it was a bit of a mad time really. Central government swooped down, rode into town, set up a task force.

UDAY: Suddenly the whole world was looking at Burnley.

ANEESA: It was like being in a goldfish bowl. We had psychologists and sociologists coming from America and Australia going up to kids playing football in the street and saying, 'What does it feel like to be growing up in Burnley?'

COLIN: And the kids were saying, 'Fuck knows, I've never been anywhere else.' There was a Task Force report by Lord Clark…he were about as much use as a chocolate fireguard…he said, 'I know what we'll do…we'll create a steering party to look at the problems.'

BELLA: The government wanted a quick fix. The weather was good...people were out on the streets in large numbers...a lot of drinking...the government thought, 'It's going to kick off again and we can't have that'...so eight thousand pounds was spent as part of 'Splash'...giving people free swims that weekend at the Thomson Centre. That did a lot to help.

ANEESA: Then SPLASH was changed to SOAR... 'Shout Out Against Racism'.

COLIN: It was going to be called Forces Against Racial Tension until they realised it spelt FART.

BELLA: The Task Force report said people in Burnley were very territorial.

COLIN: Very territorial...don't mix...yardy yardy ya...yes people in Burnley are territorial...it's a leftover from the mill culture.

BELLA: The town's like a chequerboard...each mill had like a square of streets round it, and everyone in those streets worked in that mill; and although the mills have gone it's like they're still there. The segregation here is quite shocking.

COLIN: It's not only Asian against white. It's just as much white against white, area against area.

UDAY: And there's a lot of division in the Asian Community as well.

JEN comes in with two bananas and a sandwich.

JEN: Get that down you.

BELLA: Brilliant, thanks.

JEN gives a banana to COLIN.

COLIN: Ta. What do you expect when the heart's been ripped out the place with nothing to replace it? When I was young you could pretty much stand at the top of Crown Point on the moors…you'ld have been talking thirty mills from Crown Point…

JEN: Ten mills in Padiham alone…forty along the canal…

COLIN: 'Til someone realised…send the raw materials to Pakistan, have the labour done there by 20p a day workers, and have it shipped back…it costs you less than keeping the factories open.

JEN: There's only pigeons goes in them now, and bushes growin' out chimney tops.

COLIN: And what's replaced it? Fuck all. A few shit jobs, and a lot of social workers.

BELLA: The textile industry is why people from mountain villages in Pakistan and Afghanistan came over here, and the irony is all the work's gone over there.

COLIN: While they're stuck here with fuck all to do.

JEN: People lost the sense of belonging to something. The factories weren't everyone's sense of fun, but it was like one big family, where you could share your worries. We didn't have the expectation of being doctors and nurses; didn't care how well we did at our exams; we grew up knowing we were going to be factory fodder. I started on a YOP scheme in a weaving mill, Smith and Nephews in Bryfield… I were sixteen…working nine to five…earning virtually nothing…came home and watched *Coronation Street*…too exhausted to do anything else…but they wouldn't keep me on 'cos I had… I can't spell it… Tenosynovitis…summing like that…it's a repeat strain syndrome… I were putting a lot of strain on mi wrists which really hurt and were bandaged a lot. From there I went into Dormer's, a Bedding and Sewing factory… I was a packer for curtains, and had a part-time job in a café in the market… I left to have a baby…after six weeks I went back to work in a textile factory… Northern something, oh I dunno…can't think…

BELLA: Northern and Commonwealth Fabrics.

JEN: That's it. That shut down, went bankrupt, so I moved to gold-plating bathroom fittings... 'Ultra Finishing'. I were there, had another baby...went back, I got pregnant again and got sick 'cos of the fumes in the building, so they sacked me, and the Tenosynovitis I had as a young woman got worse... I couldn't wash myself, couldn't hold the baby, couldn't feed him...very stressy, very stressy... (*Silence.*) ...got pregnant again, had number four, between three and four I'd miscarried...number four were born healthy, just after number four, marriage broke up, got a new partner pretty quick, met my husband of now, had another two children...happily married I'm pleased to say...about time. That's my life in a nutshell, but there's all sorts goes into that...lack of structure, lack of money, low aspirations...

ANEESA: Most of the girls now want to be hairdressers or work in a chippie.

UDAY: Most of the blokes want to live on the dole, but then say they want four or five kids by the time they're thirty...

ANEESA: One bloke said he wanted eleven kids...a football team...and I said, 'What, so they can grow up to be as bored as you are?'

JEN: That's a huge issue...boredom, boredom, boredom.

ANEESA: It's quite deceptive though in't it, that boredom?

JEN: How do you mean?

ANEESA: Only on the surface...there's definitely currents running underneath.

JEN: Oh yes, never ending-cycle living here...on and off the knife-edge.

BELLA: Every time someone gets arrested for supposed terrorist activity, or there's a stabbing, you're back holding your breath... 'Is it all about to kick off again?'

ANEESA: There's a whole network down there. I know a young Muslim guy, if he says, 'I want two hundred young men outside the mosque in half an hour's time', they're there. I've seen it.

BELLA: That's why Government keeps such a close eye on this place. It's got all the ingredients for something to kick off.

JEN: The council have just applied for another thirty thousand to tackle 'Extremism in Burnley'.

COLIN: Everyone's tackling something in Burnley.

BELLA: You can be an Outreach Worker, a Detached Worker, A Sexual Health Worker…

A car horn toots several times.

JEN: A Youth and Community Worker…there's Len with the cakes.

COLIN: Sarfraz…take that speaker to the van and bring the other one…

SARFRAZ: Got you.

JEN exits with TAMSIN, KYLIE, AFTAB, and SARFRAZ who takes the dud speaker.

BELLA: If you get the *Guardian* on Social and Community Opportunities Day, you'll see them all listed… Youth and Community Worker, an Information and Advisory Worker, an Inter-Agency Worker…Education Liaison Officer… there's a new one I saw listed recently… Enrichment Officer.

COLIN: What the fuck's an Enrichment Officer?

BELLA: You can be a Community Cohesion Worker. I don't know if I'm allowed to say this. After the riots which you're not allowed to call riots, the Task Force sent a sub-unit of three Community Cohesion Workers from Central Government…they asked me to do some work with young people about what they really thought, so I gave them some graffiti boards and filming equipment…a lot of the images they came up with were very violent, shockingly violent…and the response to that became the basis of my work in the town. The sort of work that Trish and I do.

TRISH back in.

TRISH: (*Quietly to BELLA.*) I've had a word with Wendy. Something's not right. She's not her usual chirpy self.

BELLA: Should we be worried?

TRISH: I think we should a bit. She says she'll talk to me later.

BELLA: Right. (*To visitors.*) Trish and I were thrown together really.

TRISH: When I transferred to Burnley I didn't come up with an agenda straightaway. I thought 'One…assess, two…look at the needs, and only then, three…take action.' My overall impression was that the town had lost its confidence…it needed someone to come in and tackle some of the negativity. And there was a lot of negative thinking between the Asian community and the white community as well…mistrust and division on both sides…so I literally wanted to mix things up.

BELLA: Trish decided to set up a group…for young people… the first properly mixed group in Burnley.

TRISH: Start at the roots…that's what you have to do. Take an individual negative and turn it into a positive. It doesn't only affect them, but all the people round them. Do you see what I'm saying? The Ripple Effect. Now, would any of you like cake? Home made.

BELLA: Not for me.

COLIN: I'll have a bit of cake if you're offering.

TRISH: Right. Anyone else? (*To visitors.*) This group…most of the people who come to it have had chaotic lifestyles… and the key workers who have ended up helping run it… Uday, Aneesa, Colin…have had to overcome real challenges in their own lives…not what you might call flimsy or superficial, but major challenges. They've all got a story.

TRISH leaves.

COLIN: She's right. Most people wouldn't touch us with a shitty stick.

UDAY: I'm the last person you'd expect to end up in youth work.

ANEESA: Or me. At one stage I never thought I'd end up with a worthwhile job. My eldest sister…this is literally how her life went…school 'til she was sixteen, job from 16 to 19, packing up bottles of bleach on a conveyor belt, then off to Pakistan into an arranged marriage to her first cousin, came back, went through the palaver of getting him British Citizenship and had her first child within ten months of being married.

COLIN: When I were six, mi mum and dad split up, mum found a new partner… Terry Havlin…yeah, as of Friday afternoon, the late Terry Havlin…after ten months he moved in with us, and a big downward spiral started.

ANEESA: And yes, that is how it was going to be for me…school, bleach, marriage…no chance of further education…that's your life…bang…no questions asked.

COLIN: Terry was a big whiskey drinker, knock Mum about… me and Lenny tried defending her; we'd get a good crack…we were covered in bruises; he'd say we'd fell out trees and stuff; he'd grab us by the privates and squeeze 'em…it would now be classed as sexual abuse. To admit that to yourself is quite strange…it's quite a…it's quite shocking.

UDAY: In my case, I had this huge anger. I was having fights in and out of school. Maybe it was the weed… I was only twelve years old when I started smoking skunk. Maybe it was the injustice in the way I was treated at school. One morning, this is God's honest truth, I walked into the science room and I yawned…that's all… I yawned, and the teacher said, 'Out…get out…you do not come into school with that attitude.' The Head of Year came to me. Do you know what he said? He said, 'Above the others' heads is clear blue sky; above your head is thunder and lightning.'

TAMSIN comes in eating cake.

TAMSIN: How long before we start? Do you want them back in?

BELLA: Ten minutes Tamsin…let's have everyone back in ten minutes. Tamsin's got a foot in both camps…she's assistant director, and she's in the play as well.

TAMSIN: And I'm learning to drive.

BELLA: And she's learning to drive so she can help out with the minibus.

TAMSIN goes. JAVED comes in with MAUREEN.

JAVED: Did you say Maureen can't watch?

BELLA: I don't think it's a good idea.

JAVED: How come this lot can watch and Maureen can't?

BELLA: They've come to observe, and be supportive. And to be blunt Javed, she's been quite disruptive in the past…

MAUREEN: No I've not.

BELLA: I'm sorry Maureen, but you've given more notes than I have.

MAUREEN: I only tell Javed when he's doing it right.

TAMSIN: (*Off.*) Ten minutes…everyone back in ten minutes.

BELLA: And you quite often take phone calls in the middle of scenes. It doesn't help group concentration.

JAVED: I've not seen her do that.

BELLA: All I'm saying is she's been quite disruptive, and I need 100 per cent concentration today. She can come tomorrow…you'll be more than welcome tomorrow. Now can you check your props please, I want to start in about ten minutes.

MAUREEN: Javed. I want a word with you outside.

MAUREEN goes. JAVED follows.

ANEESA: We weren't encouraged to do our homework.

COLIN: When I were living with mi mum, I got into the habit of not doing mi homework.

ANEESA: You're going into an arranged marriage as soon as possible…your life will be bringing up children and looking after your own parents and your husband's parents…what do you need education for?

COLIN: You'ld come home, toss your books under the stairs, get changed if you could be arsed, and then go out with your mates. I didn't give a shit, and the only thing on mi mum's mind was where the next bottle of whiskey were coming from, so she didn't give a shit either.

TRISH comes in with a piece of sponge cake on a paper plate. AFTAB follows her. He is eating a piece of cake.

TRISH: I told you they had a story. It's a sort of nutty and ginger thing, is that alright?

COLIN: Great. Ta.

TRISH: Anyone else while I'm at it?

UDAY: We're fine thanks.

TRISH: Right. Did you say ten minutes?

BELLA: Ten minutes at the most. And if they've finished eating they could start getting back into costume.

TRISH: Did you hear that everybody? You've got ten minutes to finish up and get back into costume and then you need to move back into the auditorium. Aftab, you could get into your costume now, but don't get cake on it.

AFTAB: Right.

TRISH goes back to the kitchen. AFTAB goes to the dressing room.

BELLA: Has the other speaker arrived?

COLIN: Sarfraz?

SARFRAZ: (*Off.*) Yeah?

COLIN: Is the other speaker here?

SARFRAZ: (*Off.*) Yeah. Minute.

COLIN: Fine.

ANEESA: After school and mosque, we'd just play outside… kick the can, doss on street corners, there was no curfew… obviously if I got home at midnight, she'd leather me.

UDAY: Midnight…we were out, my mate and I…it was kind of dead, all the lights were off, people were sleeping and that. We heard screaming…looked up the top of the street, two English lads, obviously drunk…we said, 'OK lads, just keep it down, people are trying to sleep, just quiet man.' They said, 'Alright, alright', walked a block down, and started shouting, 'Paki bastards.' We thought, 'We're not taking this shit in our area.' We caught up with them. The bigger English guy, after I'd given him two or three hits, he looked like he was going to sleep. The other guy came at me, so I just ducked, punched him in the stomach and pushed him away, and they kept their distance. I thought 'We've made it clear to 'em.'

A week or two later, same two lads, I was with a different lad…same sort of thing…them shouting 'Paki bastards'. We let 'em walk, don't say nothing, followed them, came to a subway, in this subway there was this graffiti… 'BNP RULES' and 'ISLAM IS BACKWARDS'.

We thought, 'Listen, let's see what we can do.' We went home. My friend got a baseball bat, I had a knife…when I talk about it now it sounds really stupid, it was almost stupid…and we decided we would go up to that subway and just sit there, see if anyone would say anything to us, and a few people walked past…and then this same white lad and his mate walked past…and I says to my mate, 'Ask him for a light.' So he turns round and says, 'Excuse me have you got a light?' and I could see the English lad had a lit cig in his hand half-smoked, and he said, 'No, I don't have a light.' I said, 'How did you spark your cig up if you don't have a light?' I said, 'He's lying to us.' He started walking up. I said, 'What do you think of the graffiti here…do you agree with it or not? What do you think of 'ISLAM IS BACKWARDS'?' He said, 'Well it is isn't it.' I said, 'Do you know the first thing about Islam? What does any religion have as its first principle? It's about peace, and treating each other well.' I said, 'Are you saying it's backwards and writing this stuff on subway walls?' He said, 'I didn't write it.' I said, 'You didn't write it, but you agree with it.' He said, 'Do you not get it? You are backwards.'

I looked at my mate through hands like this… (*Spread out like the bars of a cage over his face.*) … I went forward… I stepped ahead, and we sandwiched them to stop them going past me. I pulled my knife out, and they started shitting themselves, and my mate pulled his baseball bat out of his jacket. It was like a movie…he took a big swing…one of them ducked and he hit the other guy right on the side of his forehead…he hit him so hard the baseball bat broke. I just heard like a sickening noise; his mouth opened like he was trying to speak, but the words wouldn't form…there were just this noise like a tyre being deflated. As soon as he fell to the floor, this bruise…it was the quickest forming bruise ever… came out like half a plum stuck on the side of his head. I didn't see him awake after that. I thought, 'Whoa man.' It shocked me. I thought, 'What the hell have we done?' But I was still angry. The other guy tried walking past me, he swung for me, I ducked and I grabbed him by the collar, and I said, 'This knife could go through your neck, your face or even your chest' and I flung him to his mate who was unconscious on the floor. My mate whacked him with the broken half of the baseball bat, but bits like splinters were flying off it so it was kind of funny… I said, 'We need to get out of here,

people could come at any second...we need to get out.'
My mate picked up the two halves of the baseball bat and
we walked off quite fast, and he threw the baseball bat in a
small river like, and then we ran. It had got more serious...
it had got a lot more...phooo-ooor...what a day.

COLIN: One night Terry broke Mum's nose...she were sat
there with blood pouring down her face... I just went
absolutely mental...attacked him with everything I could
find...fists to start with, then we had these bunk beds
with metal ladders to climb in with, I hit him with the
ladders...he cracked me... I got a good hiding, ran off to
Nan and Grandad's...it was Christmas Eve...went home
later, all the doors were locked, so I hammered on the
door, and Terry opened the window...he said, 'You ran off
to your nan's...you can fucking well live there.' I shouted
for Mum, and she came to window with a cloth over her
face, and she defended Terry 'cos I'd attacked him, and
chucked me out the house... 'Go and live with Nan sort of
thing'...and it was Christmas Eve...cracking.

ANEESA: My second oldest sister was the one who fought
for an education...massive hoo-hah at home...shouting,
screaming, swearing...you'd think she'd come home and
said she'd got pregnant...my brothers joining in...it was mi
brothers that scared us more than mi mum and dad...not
just elder brothers, but younger brothers as well. They
saw it as their duty to uphold the family honour, and that
meant no stepping out of line. That's the biggest thing
which lets our community down... 'What would people
think if you step one hairsbreadth out of line?' Mi mum's
line was, 'Where did I go wrong? Why does this always
happen to me?' Mi father said mi sister was betraying the
whole family.

UDAY: I was known as Cock of the Year at school...one of the
guys we beat up had been in the year above me, knew my
name...he rang the police, who phoned the school...the
same science teacher who threw me out for yawning gave
my details to the police... I walked home the day after,

and there were about a hundred people stood outside my house…three police cars and a riot van. I took a detour off my street, and rang home, and they said, 'Where are you? Where are you?' I flagged down a police car. I said, 'Who are you looking for?' They said, 'Taz Uday.' I said, 'That's me.'

COLIN: I ended up living with Nan and Granddad, and they got me to do my homework; and I joined a local youth club, and a snooker club. Mi granddad saved up and bought me a cue.

ANEESA: By sheer doggedness, mi sister won in the end. She went to Leeds University to study psychology. My next sister, instead of saying, 'I want to go to University' she said, 'I am going to University.' By the time it got to me, my parents said, 'You will go to University, and you will read psychology'…mi father all proud going round telling people, 'Oh mi daughter's gone to University. We're a very progressive family.' Though mi elder sister who started it off…she's a University lecturer now… she's got a great career…but because she's thirty-seven and not married, people say she must be either mad, a witch or a pervert.

COLIN: I got five Cs and two Bs in GCSEs.

ANEESA: I got my psychology degree.

UDAY: I got a two-year custodial sentence.

COLIN: I wanted to be an RAF pilot…'cos my favourite film is *Top Gun*… I watched it every morning of school holidays for six weeks…quite sad really…but the next summer the youth club leader said, 'I want you to be a worker… 25 hours a week, and I'll give you some more hours if you come in in the morning, and give the place a sweep, a mop, and a general vac.' And I started doing volunteer work, like organising trips to Blackpool for the kids who are not looked after so well.

ANEESA: I decided to jack it in…psychology…it wasn't what I wanted to do with my life, and I volunteered as a community worker. Then I got this call from Trish.

UDAY: I first met Trish when I was still fighting and smoking weed…one of the youth workers introduced me…she said, 'Hiya, I'm Trish.' She put her hand out, she said, 'How would you like to start a project with me…no one knows anything about it yet, but hopefully it'll stir things up a bit…and you're just the sort of person I need.'

COLIN: I was at the snooker club…Riley's…one night… I'm quite good, my highest break is 49…there are lads who can knock in 110 breaks with their eyes shut, cocky bastards, and I got this phone call from a woman called Trish…

UDAY: Two days after I got inside prison, I got a postcard…it was from Trish. 'Hello Uday, just heard the sad news…' I've still got it at home… 'Letting you know we're thinking of you, and we're here for you every step, and we'll be here waiting for you when you get out.'

COLIN: The very first meeting the group was nameless, and then we had a brain-storming session…oh sorry, you're not allowed to say that anymore…it in't politically correct… have to say 'thought shower' 'cos if you're epileptic and you go into a fit, it's known as a brain storm, so people at the Council who think up all this bollocks, think that if you or me says 'brain storm', all the epileptics are going to throw their arms up in horror. Same as blackboard…have to call 'em chalkboards 'cos some fuckwit thinks someone might be offended.

The kids came up with…loads of names were suggested… two young lads basically came up with 'Street YY'…the 'wise' bit spelt with two capital Ys, for Asian Youth and White youth.

KYLIE: (*Off.*) She says you're not to go in / there, bitch!

MAUREEN: (*Off.*) I'll go where I fucking well want.

JAVED, MAUREEN, KYLIE, TAMSIN come back in.

BELLA: Hey, what's going on?

MAUREEN: Get yer hands off me you slag.

KYLIE: I'll bang you out.

BELLA: Oy, you two, calm down.

KYLIE: I'm going for a fag.

KYLIE exits.

BELLA: Don't be long. Have you checked your props?

JEN comes in from the kitchen.

JEN: What's going on?

BELLA: Don't ask me.

JAVED: I'm being exploited in this part; you know that, don't you?

BELLA: What do you mean by that?

MAUREEN: 'Cos he is. You know he is.

JEN: That salad's getting dried up.

BELLA: I think if you recall…it was you wanted the part.

JAVED: I'm the only proper Asian guy you could get.

BELLA: We've got Aftab and Uday.

JAVED: I'm the only one with the requisite skills, and I'm not being appreciated.

BELLA: It's a team effort.

JEN: You should listen to that. Good advice.

JEN heads back towards the kitchen with the salad.

MAUREEN: (*After her.*) Told yer no-one would eat it.

JEN: (*Going.*) Have to keep trying though, don't yer?

JAVED: What'll you do if I walk out?

MAUREEN: Come on, let's go.

BELLA: We're meant to be starting. Where's your jacket...your Rikki Rajah jacket?

MAUREEN: I've told him not to wear it. It makes him look gay.

BELLA: He's a television presenter. He's meant to look gay.

MAUREEN: I don't like it. He should wear his leather jacket.

BELLA: I'm sorry Maureen, I'm the director of this play, and I say he should wear the Rikki Rajah jacket.

MAUREEN: I think you should walk out.

JAVED: I might just do that. Then what are you going to do?

MAUREEN: We'll make a decision and let you know. Javed... outside...now!

BELLA: We haven't got time for all this.

MAUREEN and JAVED walk out. SARFRAZ comes back in with a different loudspeaker. COLIN helps him wire it up. AFTAB comes back in, in his costume for the play.

TAMSIN: Don't worry. He'll be back. We've seen it all before.

BELLA: How long are you two gonna be?

COLIN: Two minutes...three minutes tops.

BELLA: How this play came about...what happened... I'd heard about a community project in Belfast called 'The Wedding Play'...a promenade piece looking at Catholics and Protestants...

TAMSIN: There was an idea we should do something similar here about whites and Asians.

BELLA: Trish took it on, did the fundraising for it, and asked me to direct it... and then we had a two-day residential to discuss how to put the play together.

AFTAB: I was sat there looking at my watch.

SARFRAZ: They were having this very boring conversation about mixed relationships.

AFTAB: Very boring, with an exclamation mark as well.

TAMSIN: Javed was determined to get his own point of view across…he said the only way would be for the guy to be Asian and the girl to be white and for them both to end up dead.

BELLA: Javed wanted it to be a Romeo and Juliet thing, with him playing Romeo of course. Every time anyone does a play about Burnley, they want it to be a Romeo and Juliet thing.

TAMSIN: I said I thought it showed the divisions…even within Street YY…the Asian lads stay with the Asian lads… I stay with the white girls. Trish is always trying to mix it up…we do warm-ups where you have to go and ask someone a question you don't know about them, but it doesn't seem to make that much difference.

BELLA: All the more reason to look at the whole subject.

UDAY: I didn't agree with promoting mixed relationships…it's not our right to tell people 'Mix, mix, mix.' Doing a play about it makes it look like if you're going out with someone of your own background it's OK, if you're going out in a mixed relationship that's somehow superior, and that's a bollocks way of looking at it.

BELLA: I don't remember anyone saying that…or even suggesting it…we merely said we wanted all young people to have choices. After the discussion, what happened…the kids did some research. They did a series of interviews with some friends of mine called Catherine and Bilal who are in a mixed relationship. We wanted to look at the subject, in a not too serious way, but one which would raise a lot of questions… so we came up with a TV show called it *The Rikki Rajah Show*, with this flash Asian compere called Rikki Rajah to link the whole thing together…a sort of Indian Graham Norton…and it's a bit like *Blind Date*. This young Asian man played by Aftab has to choose one of three white girls to go on a holiday to Australia with.

COLIN goes back to the lighting box.

Anyway, we started rehearsals in March.

TAMSIN: After Easter, Trish and Bella asked everyone who'd been at the meeting if they'd like to be in the play, and I said 'Yes.' We did a couple of weeks of role playing, and I got the part of the make-up artist, one of the Bollywood-type dancers, and agreed to be assistant director as well. I'd never done acting before except I played a donkey in a Nativity play... I was the back end.

BELLA: I have to say rehearsal's not been easy. I don't think I've had a single rehearsal with a full cast.

TAMSIN: You were never going to get many Asian girls...

ANEESA: And of course, if they do come, the parents don't know. It's something I'd do...lie...sneak off.

BELLA: Three Asian girls came to the residential...it was only when we were coming back I found out they'd snuck out...forged the parents' signatures.

ANEESA: There's no way Asian parents are going to let them out if it's a mixed group...the whole idea of mixing with young white people means decadence and depravity...and if theatricals were involved...well...you might as well sell your soul to the devil.

UDAY: Most of the Asian lads won't do acting because they think it's gay.

TAMSIN: White lads of a certain age don't want to come. They just want to get pissed and stoned.

ANEESA: Asians that get involved are called 'Coconuts'.

UDAY: And white girls that come along are called Paki-shaggers.

BELLA: There have been mixed relationships within the group, which does bring its own difficulties. Not just Javed and Maureen... Aftab and Wendy have been going out, and

Tamsin won't mind me saying, but she's been in a mixed relationship, haven't you, and it's not all been plain sailing.

TAMSIN: I met Jari through a friend of a friend. He chatted me up the whole time… 'Please give me your number.' He really was the nicest person you could ever meet. On Valentine's Day, Bella dropped me off to him, and he bought me a big bunch of red roses. He'd buy me teddies, and little key-rings with 'my girlfriend' on the tab. We'd go to the cinema… I don't know…we did nothing and everything…be a couple…go for a walk in the park in the sun, hand in hand…but then in town he'd be like 'Oh shit, mi dad's mates' and I'd be like, 'Well, they've seen us now anyway' and he'd be like, 'Let go of mi hand.'

AFTAB: If any of our Asian lads go with a white girl they keep it quiet from their parents. Otherwise it's slipper off…get a beating. My mum won't allow me to bring Wendy into the house. I don't talk about her to my family.

TAMSIN: And thinking back I'm like…no wonder…because he's a dirty lying dog.

There were all these girlfriends. One day I went through his phone and I found a video with a girl on the bed completely naked, with him in the background going, 'Baby, baby, oh Cindy' he said to her 'Oh Cindy, Cindy, I'm gonna bounce your ass like you've got hydraulics in your G-string.'

BELLA: I need a wee before we start. Are you set up Colin?

COLIN: I'm fine.

BELLA: Is that speaker working yet?

SARFRAZ: Should be. Try it.

BELLA: Are you two ready?

ANEESA: We need to get changed.

BELLA: You've not got long. Tamsin, how's the programme?

TAMSIN: It seems fine to me.

BELLA: Uday, will you phone Len and say that's fine…print off two hundred.

UDAY: I'll do that now.

BELLA goes. UDAY and ANEESA go to the dressing room. COLIN puts a burst of music through the speaker.

COLIN: That's fine. I need a piss an' all.

COLIN goes.

TAMSIN: He didn't like me seeing his friends, because he thought I might go off with one of them, so he'd always fetch the ones who couldn't speak much English, but the ones who could speak English would come up to me in the nightclub and say, 'Jari's married. He's telling us not to tell ya, but he is.' So I asked him, and he said, 'No, no, I do have a child, and I did have a wife from India, but she lives in Manchester now. We got a divorce, because she treated my mum real bad.' He used to come every day to collect me when I had to go to work. I'd be in the shower, and he sat downstairs with mi mum having tea and toast, and mi mum was, 'Yeah, he's that nice; I think he has changed for the better.' Obviously not…idiot…'cos in the end it turned out he was married. His real wife is an Asian lady not from India but from Bangladesh, arranged marriage, living here in Burnley. She'd come all the way from Bangladesh to make life with a complete bastard. Oh and the flash BMW with the alloy wheels he used to drive me round in…that turned out to be stolen…and he was part of a drug-selling ring in Leicester…and he had a child with a woman in Wolverhampton, and screwed my best friend, but apart from that he was the perfect boyfriend really. I wish I'd listened to people now… I did love him to begin with…but if that's what boyfriends are like I never want another one in my life… Now they can all have him…share him…

AFTAB: I've already met the girl in Bangladesh I'm supposed to marry. I do love Wendy, but it's not realistic in the long term. My long-term plans… I'll marry this Bangladeshi woman who can just come in and cook for me…couldn't be white 'cos she wouldn't be able to cook the Asian way. The main thing will be to help look after my parents… and we'll have kids. But if I'm being really honest, I'm probably like all the others and I might have a side-dish if you know what I mean…could be either Asian or white or Spanish.

TAMSIN: That's what they do.

AFTAB: Have a play with the ladies outside, go home, ask their wife for a massage, and go to sleep.

TAMSIN: Poor wife. Half these guys have got sexually transmitted diseases. 'New English word learned today… Chlamydia…what does it mean?'

BELLA: (*Off.*) I want to start now…everyone back in. And if you're not already into costume, do it now.

TAMSIN: I need to get changed…sorry.

TAMSIN exits. KYLIE enters in her Bollywood dancer costume.

SARFRAZ: The girls in Burnley, specially the English girls, they're all over us Asian boys. You should see them man; you talk to them for like five minutes and offer them a cigarette, they're just like, 'You want a blow job?'

KYLIE: A lot of lasses give the Asian lads a blow job for the drugs. I just do it 'cos I like it.

SARFRAZ: It's too easy man. I've stopped going in for all that shit.

AFTAB: When he gets a blow job, he steals their knickers, puts them in his wardrobe.

SARFRAZ: What you laughing at?

AFTAB: If you go to his bottom wardrobe, it's full of knickers. He's got Kylie's knickers as well.

KYLIE: No he fucking hasn't.

AFTAB: He has. Such a weirdo.

SARFRAZ: Me the weirdo, you fat Bungi bitch.

KYLIE: What are they like then?

AFTAB: Very flashy, funky, like curtain nets. If you ever get hungry, you can catch a fish with them.

KYLIE: You're talking through your fucking arse.

AFTAB: So what about the Rhode Island Coffee shop?

KYLIE: What about it?

AFTAB: Has he phoned you?

SARFRAZ: I haven't heard this. What's this?

AFTAB: We were in the Rhode Island Coffee shop yesterday, and we were asking Kylie what her score was...

SARFRAZ: Lost count...

AFTAB: And she said... 'Whatever it is, it's about to be one more.' And there was this Asian bloke on the pavement looking in through the window...

SARFRAZ: Too easy.

KYLIE: He were better looking than you two put together.

AFTAB: She's straight out... 'Here's mi phone number...gi'us a ring'.

KYLIE: Only a phone number.

AFTAB: Has he phoned you?

KYLIE: I told him I was busy today.

SARFRAZ: If you really fancy a white girl, and she's proving a bit hard to get, you can take her out for a meal, cinema, club in Manchester, taxi home...hundred pounds minimum; but why do all that when you can get her on 'The / Magic Roundabout'?

AFTAB: 'The Magic Roundabout'.

SARFRAZ: It costs exactly one pound ten p. White girls...they love White Lightning cider...it costs one pound nine p.

AFTAB: And you use the penny for a penny sweet.

SARFRAZ: After five or six sips, they're already on the way, but you let them drink the whole thing, and then you look deep into their eyes, and you can see that they're on 'The Magic Roundabout', and they get really jiggy.

AFTAB: And if you set your mobile phone to video you've got a free porn movie as well.

SARFRAZ: And then you give them the penny sweet after as a reward. I'll tell you something…this is what mixed relationships are like in real life.

AFTAB: But none of this is / in the play.

SARFRAZ: None of this is in the play.

BELLA comes back in.

BELLA: Where is everyone? There's no-one here.

KYLIE: Full run through?

BELLA: Dress rehearsal, Kylie, it's called a dress rehearsal.

COLIN and SARFRAZ enter with ANEESA and UDAY who are now in costume.

Come on, come on. Uday, what have you got on under that T-shirt ?

UDAY: A white T-shirt.

BELLA: So you're wearing two T-shirts?

UDAY: Do you want me to change it?

BELLA: No, just don't wear it tomorrow. Kylie, have you seen Javed?

KYLIE: They're sitting in the bus shelter.

BELLA: Well could you go and get him…quickly…we need to get going.

KYLIE runs off.

Colin, are you all set up?

COLIN: Fine. I'm going to let Sarfraz do the lights, so he gets used to it.

BELLA: Right. Good luck Sarfraz.

TRISH enters with WENDY who is now in costume.

TRISH: Sure you alright?

WENDY: I'll be fine.

TRISH: We'll talk later.

AFTAB: Are you alright?

WENDY: Yeah, I'll be OK.

AFTAB: We were a bit worried.

WENDY: I know.

AFTAB: Nervous?

WENDY: It's not that. I'm not feeling great that's all.

BELLA: Come on, come on, can you all hurry up please.

TAMSIN, KYLIE, and JAVED enter.

Right…at last. Let's get started. This is a full dress rehearsal.

TRISH: Did you all hear that? This is a full dress rehearsal.

BELLA: This means you won't get a prompt for your lines. You know your lines. We did that speed run on Wednesday… are you listening?…so I know you know them. Try and remember them; and if you forget them, try and help each other out.

TRISH: I saw at least three people talking back there.

BELLA: I want you to imagine this is tomorrow…the audience is full of people. Act your best…remember your characters, and remember the status work we did last week.

TRISH: I think there's still talking. What's the last words Bella said? Anybody?

WENDY: Think about the character work you've done.

KYLIE: No, no…help each other out she said.

WENDY: Yeah, yeah, and the character work.

KYLIE: Alright dickhead.

TRISH: And that doesn't mean noise backstage does it.

BELLA: OK standby everyone…everyone ready with the lights?

COLIN: Do you want the tape running?

BELLA: I want the lights and music together. Can you do that Sarfraz?

SARFRAZ: Now?

BELLA: I'll give you the thumbs up. OK the audience are all in now…

MAUREEN walks in and sits in the audience.

TRISH: I'm sorry Maureen, but I think this is inappropriate.

JAVED: I've told her she can sit in on the rehearsal.

MAUREEN: That was our decision. Either I sit here or he goes.

BELLA: Well she can't.

MAUREEN: Are you lot jealous or what?

TRISH: How do you mean?

MAUREEN: I've seen the way you look at me. Are you lezzers or what?

TRISH: I don't mean to be rude, but I think you should leave.

KYLIE: You're the fucking lezzer.

TRISH: Language Kylie please.

MAUREEN: Is your phone on?

JAVED: Yes.

MAUREEN: Right. Don't switch it off. I will ring you when I'm outside.

MAUREEN storms out.

BELLA: Can you all get in your opening positions. Ready Sarfraz?

KYLIE: Oooh, look, Wendy in a skirt. She'll be wearing lipstick next.

BELLA: Kylie, shut up. Opening positions, and…

BELLA gives the thumbs up. Music and flashing lights.

The girls adopt the poses of dancers in a Bollywood movie.

The girls gyrate their hips.

JAVED sashays to the front of the stage wearing his Rikki Rajah jacket.

The girls do their dance routine and end up singing 'Welcome to the Rikki Rajah Show.'

TAMSIN puts a jacket over her dress. UDAY brings on a towel and a chair. ANEESA holds a mirror.

TAMSIN: We're ready for you Mr Rajah.

JAVED walks to the chair. UDAY takes his jacket. JAVED sits down.

UDAY puts a towel round his shoulders.

UDAY: Can I fetch you anything Mr Rajah?

JAVED: Mineral water with a dash of lime, plenty of ice.

UDAY: Certainly Mr Rajah.

JAVED: And dim the lights a little, yaar. I've a headache this morning.

UDAY: Yes Mr Rajah.

UDAY pretends to switch a light. All the lights go out.

SARFRAZ: (*Quietly.*) Motherfucker. (*Loud.*) Sorry everyone.

The lights come back on.

TAMSIN: I'll start with a little base Mr Rajah…it'll bring out your cheekbones.

KYLIE comes on with a clipboard.

KYLIE: Ten minutes til we're on air. Ten minutes everybody.

KYLIE exits.

JAVED: You'll have to do something about my eyes. They're looking a little tired. I have to charm the nation with these eyes, yaar… I bring a ray of sunshine into the…into the…living rooms of the…

TAMSIN: (*Sotto voce.*) Punters…

JAVED: Punters, up and down the land.

TAMSIN: And I think a little blusher on the cheeks, for that something extra.

His mobile phone rings.

JAVED: (*On phone.*) Yes? Why?

TAMSIN: (*Quietly.*) That's not…

JAVED: I said why. Yes.

ANEESA: (*To BELLA.*) I don't know…

JAVED: Right. (*Switches off phone. Shouts.*) RIGHT…I'M OFF! I'm off.

TAMSIN: Bella…

JAVED: I don't want to do your play, I can't be arsed with you people, and I'm going. And tell you what pleases me. Because it's so late in the day and I'm playing the main part, you won't be able to find anyone else to learn the lines.

BELLA: I don't like to point this out, but you're the only one who doesn't know his lines.

JAVED: I don't care. You'll have to cancel, and I'm pleased. I'm really pleased.

JAVED goes.

BELLA: I don't believe this. Sarfraz, could you put the house lights up.

All the lights go out.

SARFRAZ: Motherfucker.

The lights come on.

BELLA: I just don't believe this.

WENDY and AFTAB come from the back.

AFTAB: What's going on?

ANEESA: Javed's walked out.

AFTAB: Has he really walked out?

ANEESA: Looks like he has.

TAMSIN: Shall I go after him?

UDAY: I'll go.

TRISH: No. I'll go.

KYLIE comes on.

KYLIE: Has he really gone?

UDAY: He says he has.

TRISH: I'll go and have a word.

TRISH exits.

AFTAB: He'll be back in a minute.

BELLA: He always has before.

KYLIE: I don't want him back.

WENDY: I don't want him back.

TAMSIN: We can't do the play without him.

KYLIE: No, fuck him, and his lezzy bitch.

BELLA: Tamsin's right...we can't do the play without him.

ANEESA: Uday can play his part.

UDAY: No way. There's no way.

ANEESA: You can take the script on. Read the lines. No-one'll mind.

UDAY: No way. I'm happy to play the attendant, but I'm not doing all that.

JEN comes in. SARFRAZ comes down from the lighting panel.

JEN: Javed's just left with Maureen. He says he's not coming back.

BELLA: Slight crisis.

COLIN: Major crisis.

JEN: What are you going to do?

ANEESA: Aftab.

AFTAB: You must be joking. I can't sing and I can't dance.

TRISH comes back in.

TRISH: Not good. They seem to have left. I can't see them anywhere.

AFTAB: I'll try phoning.

BELLA: We can't do anything without him.

SARFRAZ: I'll do it.

TRISH: What do you mean?

SARFRAZ: I'll be wicked man. I could be a stand-up comic me. I can make people laugh. (*AFTAB laughs.*) See. I've made him laugh already.

TRISH: It's very nice of you to offer.

SARFRAZ: What? No. I'm not getting up on any fucking stage man. I'm not gay.

TRISH: I thought you were offering.

SARFRAZ: No. You have to be mad to go out there.

AFTAB: (*Signals for everyone to be quiet.*) Hi man…it's Aftab…we were wondering… have you really gone, or is it…right… right… OK…yeah, cool man…bye.

No he's really gone.

COLIN: Fuck this for a game of soldiers.

BELLA: I don't believe it. He certainly picks his moments.

TRISH: What are we going to do?

BELLA: What's the time now?

TRISH: What is the time?

COLIN: Half five.

BELLA: There's nothing we can do tonight. He may come back tomorrow. Did he say anything about tomorrow?

AFTAB: No, but knowing Javed, he'll be back.

BELLA: I'm sorry Trish, there's no point in doing the Dress without the main actor.

COLIN: She's right. Waste of time.

TRISH: If that's what you say…you're the expert. I would have thought we could put something together. (*To visitors.*) I don't know what you lot think. It must be very disappointing for you.

BELLA: Sorry…it'll be waste of time.

TRISH: Alright. If that's what you say.

JEN: If you want any more to eat, you'd better grab it now.

JEN goes.

KYLIE: I'm dying for a fucking fag.

WENDY: I'm quite glad he's gone.

KYLIE: How dare she call me a fucking lezzer. She's (*WENDY.*) the only lezzer round here.

WENDY is visibly upset, and after a few moments walks to the armchair.

BELLA: Will you all go and get changed now. Hang your costumes up neatly.

TRISH: Did you hear that? Hang them up neatly.

BELLA: Aftab…where are you going?

AFTAB: Game of Fußball?

BELLA: No. Go and get changed…you can help get the costumes into the minibus.

We'll meet in the foyer in ten minutes. (*Goes.*)

TRISH: You see the difficulties we face, but always remember…it's the process not the product. That might be a bit awkward to explain to an audience tomorrow night, but if we don't have a play, we don't have a play. We could have a question and answer session instead. The time won't be wasted I can assure you.

The others start to drift off.

UDAY: I'm sorry, I'm not singing or poncing about like that for anyone.

COLIN: He's a fuckwit.

SARFRAZ: A poodle fuckwit.

UDAY: It's that girl. She's got him wrapped round her little pinkie.

SARFRAZ: I don't know why he's so precious about her. We've all had her.

AFTAB: Not me.

SARFRAZ: That's because you're a fat greasy pooch.

KYLIE: She just wants to get her chops round his dick.

COLIN: He'll be back in five minutes and they'll all make a fucking fuss of him.

SARFRAZ: Told you. A motherfucking lapdog.

They go.

WENDY alone in the armchair. TRISH watches her.

TRISH: Now then. Do you want to talk about it?

WENDY: I don't know.

TRISH: You don't have to. I'm just asking.

WENDY: I need a Hobnob.

TRISH: Right, I'll get you one.

TRISH leaves. She comes back.

There you go. I've bought the packet.

WENDY: You know I'm normally a happy bunny.

TRISH: I would say that was true, yes.

WENDY: Monday today.

TRISH: Yes, I know.

WENDY: Friday night, I was raped on the way home.

TRISH: I knew it was serious. Do you want to tell me about it?

WENDY: He bashed mi head against a wall… I tried to move…he bashed it again, said if I tried to move, next time it would be really hard.

TRISH: Where was this?

WENDY: Just round the corner from where I live.

TRISH: You've no idea who?

WENDY: White guy, about seventeen…eighteen…never seen him before.

TRISH: Have you told the police?

WENDY: No.

TRISH: Because of the other business?

WENDY: Yes.

TRISH: You've not told Aftab?

WENDY: No.

TRISH: 'Cos I think he's concerned.

WENDY: Only you.

TRISH: You've not told yer mum?

WENDY: No.

TRISH: Stupid question really.

WENDY: Yes.

COLIN comes on.

COLIN: Sorry to interrupt…

TRISH: That's alright.

COLIN: Could you move your car…it's blocking in the van…

TRISH: Here are mi keys.

COLIN takes the keys and goes. TRISH sits and listens to WENDY.

WENDY: My mother…in my phone…if you look on my mobile phone…it comes up as 'The Mother' is calling… that's what she is… 'The Mother'. I live with my mother… she doesn't have much time for me. I don't talk to anyone at home…my sister's a bitch…as long as I've got my music on I'm fine. When I'm told to turn it down I get annoyed.

In January, Aftab, now he's my boyfriend, he just said, 'Come along to "Street YY",' 'cos he knew I liked drama. I was a bit quiet at the start, but then I had to get up and act in a scene, so I just let rip…it was like a white couple, an Asian couple, and a mixed couple at home, and we had to act how we thought it was. We weren't being really sarcastic…but for the Asian couple we put on an Asian accent and asked for chapattis.

I felt good when I got home… I liked the fact that I didn't have to sit alone in my room and just think why shit happens to me and it doesn't happen to anyone else. I've

70

got to the stage where I'd like a mum, but not my mother, 'cos I don't like the person she is.

I'm banned from Aftab's house 'cos his mother doesn't like the age gap…he's twenty… I'm sixteen…that's what she says anyway; and my mum, she said, 'It's got to end, that's my opinion' she said 'and it's all Trish Benyon's fault,' she said, ''cos she's a meddling do-gooder.'

I didn't tell anyone about the rape 'til now. It brought lots up from my past which is extremely difficult to deal with… 'cos of what he did…my mum's ex-boyfriend…when I was seven 'til twelve…not all the time, but whenever he could find his chance…he wasn't fussy where he put it…not just physical abuse…emotional and mental as well. That's why I didn't go the police Friday night… I can't think about the rape without…it's a double whammy really…without thinking about all the times he did what he did. And I don't want to tell Aftab or my friends or people here…if they hug me and that…it makes me feel even more like there's something wrong with me. I just want to be my usual sarky, sparky self. That's how I'm known in the group…as being the sarky one.

TRISH: This story she's told you…you will treat it with the respect it deserves, won't you? We're very concerned about the telling of stories which make them vulnerable. And some of them are underage…you know…well underage… so we need to be vigilant…and in many ways I feel personally responsible for them…and I'll not have them exploited. You do understand that, don't you? I couldn't have children…not myself…and I know people say that makes me like a surrogate mother, but I don't see anything wrong with that. It just means I'm all the more determined they get a good start in life. Tired?

WENDY: Yeah.

TRISH: I'll give you a lift home. I think the best thing is if you have a good rest tonight and then we'll meet first thing in the morning and see where we're going from here. Does that sound good to you?

WENDY: Yeah. Thanks.

TRISH: I'll have a Hobnob if you're offering.

WENDY: Sorry.

TRISH: This is what this work is all about. This is what 'Street YY' is all about. Giving young people a solid base; breaking down the social barriers; helping them through the difficult times; raising their sights really. You'd have seen all o' that by watching them do the play. They've worked very hard at it, and they've come a long way in the last six months... I'ld say you have anyways...

WENDY: Yeah.

TRISH: Yes, I think so. This is why I'm grieved you're not seeing the play tonight, though with any luck you'll see it tomorrow. It's important. It's all part of that process of turning your life around. You look at Aneesa, and Colin, and Uday...you've heard their stories...very few people go through all that and come out the other side; people put money on Uday turning out bad. Now look at him. He's helping other young people with difficult situations, and doing it brilliantly. You've got to trust people. I should know. I turned my life around. Before my conversion... I had a conversion at 16...this'll surprise you... I used to sell my body. Yes it's true. I've always had good bosoms... I used to charge the local lads... I think it was threepence I used to charge...threepence for a look and a feel, and a penny for a look at the bottom but you couldn't touch that...just a look. That was mi source of income, that and Woolworth's...with its square counter it was a gift. I'd shoplift to order. After mi conversion, I still had a lot o' things under mi bed. I packed it all up into two large bags and late at night I left it in Woolworth's doorway with a note saying, 'Sorry I pinched all this stuff... I've changed mi ways now.'

COLIN comes on. Gives TRISH her car keys back.

COLIN: Sorry…me again…have you got keys to the minibus?

TRISH: Oh yes, I have. Are you driving or Aneesa?

COLIN: Aneesa. I've got to load the van.

JEN comes on.

JEN: I've all this salad left. Do you want it?

TRISH: Truthfully no.

JEN: Either of you?

COLIN: No thanks.

WENDY: No thanks.

TRISH: Mi hubby won't touch it.

JEN: Nor mine.

JEN goes.

TRISH: Will you be in later?

COLIN: Bound to be.

TRISH: I'll call you about tomorrow.

BELLA comes on.

BELLA: They're all waiting by the minibus.

TRISH: I'll give Wendy a lift home.

BELLA: Right.

TRISH: I might drop in on you later if that's alright.

BELLA: I'll be in all evening, with mi feet up.

TRISH: See where we've got to sort o' thing.

COLIN: Don't worry. He'll be back.

COLIN goes.

BELLA: If we don't have a performance…just in case…

TRISH: Yes?

BELLA: 'Cos we interviewed them to make the play, I've just rung Bilal and Catherine, and put them on stand-by to do a question and answer session, and they've very kindly said 'yes'.

TRISH: Kick it off so to speak. Good idea. Does it have to be Catherine and Bilal?

BELLA: Why?

TRISH: It's only that Roy de Lisle says he's coming…

BELLA: Roy's coming? Right.

TRISH: There's a bit of a thing going on at the moment between him and Cath.

BELLA: What sort of thing?

TRISH: Something to do with funding. I'm not sure. They're not really talking; that's what I heard. (*To visitors.*) Roy's a county officer…that's quite a senior position. (*Back to BELLA.*) I don't want anything going pear-shaped in front of him. Who else is coming that you know?

BELLA: Most of the parents, loads o' friends. I don't think you need worry.

TRISH: No, not with that lot…it's not going to kick off is it?

BELLA: You'll be fine. And it's only a 'just in case'… I'm pretty sure the play's going to happen.

TRISH: That's true…very disappointing otherwise… I mean Len's having the programmes printed and everything.

BELLA: Javed'll be back. He'll phone me in a minute. We'll fit in a dress rehearsal in the afternoon sometime.

TRISH: He'll not want to miss out, will he? All the attention.

BELLA goes.

(*To the departing BELLA.*) Anyway…fingers crossed. Talk later.

BELLA: (*Off.*) See you.

TRISH: You'll excuse me won't you? I've got to get Wendy home. What else can I say? I'm sorry, but that's it really. You must be so disappointed. You've come all this way and we've nothing to show you. Then again, with any luck, you'll see it tomorrow, so it's not long to wait really is it? (*To WENDY.*) Where's the rest of your stuff?

WENDY: In the dressing room.

TRISH: Are you alright to go home?

WENDY: Yeah.

TRISH: And you'll be up to a performance tomorrow night, will yer?

WENDY: Yeah.

TRISH: Come on then.

TRISH sees AFTAB coming on.

I'll wait for you in the lobby.

WENDY: Right.

TRISH: (*Quietly to visitors.*) Oh well…see you tomorrow. Bye.

She goes, leaving AFTAB and WENDY together.

AFTAB: You alright?

WENDY: Yeah. I've not been feeling very well that's all. I banged mi head, that's what it was. Just there look.

AFTAB: How d'you do that?

WENDY: In the cupboard under the stairs.

AFTAB: At home?

WENDY: Yeah…stupid really. You know me.

AFTAB: I've got to stay and help. Pack the costumes and that.

WENDY: I heard.

AFTAB: I'd better go…they're waiting.

WENDY: Right. I'll see you tomorrow.

AFTAB: See you tomorrow.

They kiss tentatively…then a full blown snog.

Lights to black.

Act Two

The same community centre the following night. SARFRAZ at the lighting desk.

WENDY and AFTAB come on. AFTAB walks to the back and goes to the Fußball.

AFTAB: Top right corner…eyes closed.

> *WENDY sits on one of the chairs lined up either side of the stage.*
>
> *TRISH hurries on. She has new designer glasses. Her hair has been slightly bouffoned.*

TRISH: Has anyone seen Sarfraz?

SARFRAZ: I'm here.

TRISH: Do you think you could do some nice lighting?

SARFRAZ: Ambience.

TRISH: If you say so.

SARFRAZ: Sure.

> *UDAY and ANEESA come on and sit down on the sofa.*

TRISH: Uday, Aneesa… I thought we'd have Catherine and Bilal there. Aftab, you could take your seat now couldn't you?

> *ROY DE LISLE comes in.*

Oh look there's Roy. Evening Roy.

ROY: Hello Trish.

TRISH: So glad you could make it.

ROY: (*Private.*) Is that who I thought it was?

TRISH: (*Private.*) Where?

ROY: (*Private.*) Outside.

TRISH: (*Private.*) Yes I think it probably was. The trouble is they helped us with the play, and Bella asked them before I could do anything about it.

ROY: (*Private.*) I'll just have to grin and bear it, won't I?

TRISH: (*Private.*) This is all about the young people. I'm sure she won't say anything out of turn.

ROY: (*Private.*) I can't say I share your confidence. She's proving to be a real thorn in my flesh.

TRISH: (*Public.*) I kept you a seat over here, Roy.

TRISH shows him to a chair in the audience.

ROY: (*Seeing the visitors.*) Evening. (*Private.*) Who are they?

TRISH: (*Private.*) Friends of Bella's…writers and so on…from London…

ROY: (*Private.*) Not again.

TRISH: (*Private.*) They seem harmless enough. (*Public.*) Look, I've put you just here. Do you want a brew?

ROY: No, I've just had mi supper thanks all the same.

TRISH: See you later.

BELLA and TAMSIN usher on BILAL and CATHERINE and seat them on the sofa.

BELLA: We'll let you talk for a while and then throw it open as a general discussion.

WENDY: Hello.

CATHERINE: Hello Wendy. Hi Uday. Hi Aneesa.

BILAL: Hello Uday.

UDAY: Alright?

ANEESA: Hello.

CATHERINE: Is that Roy de Lisle in the audience?

BELLA: Er…oh yes.

CATHERINE: I didn't know he was going to be here.

BELLA: Yes, sorry about that. I asked you before I knew he was coming.

CATHERINE: Could be an interesting evening.

TRISH: Right…are we all here?

KYLIE walks in.

Kylie. (*She points to a chair at the side. KYLIE sits.*) Aftab, can you take your seat now please. I think I've asked you once already haven't I? Jen… Jen, are you going to join us?

JEN: (*From kitchen.*) No, I'm just butties and Sugar Puffs me. I'm fine in here. I'm just kitchen, me.

TRISH: No, you should join us. Jen's always good in a discussion. She says things how they are.

JEN: (*Entering.*) I'm not very PC.

TRISH: Right, Sarfraz is about to give us some nice lighting and then we'll get cracking.

UDAY: Show off your new hair-do.

TAMSIN: Bit of a makeover, one way and another.

JEN: Very swanky.

TAMSIN: I like them.

JEN: Don't be put off, Trish, they suit you.

TRISH: I didn't think anyone would notice. You know what I'm like…me with mi value system…glasses are glasses to me.

TAMSIN: Where'd they come from?

TRISH: Ted Baker. I don't know. But that's all people have said all day long… 'Trish, you've got designer glasses.' I didn't know… I just bought a pair I liked. And I checked the side for the logo, but I can't see without mi glasses, so I can't even tell if they're real. But what I like is …it goes red, then blue you know, like iridescent.

The stage is filled with purple and orange lights.

SARFRAZ: How's that?

TRISH: Can you do something a bit more neutral. Work on it while we make a start. Do you want a brew or anything?

BILAL: No, I'm fine.

TRISH: Sure?

CATHERINE: Fine.

TRISH: Right… I'm pleased to see at least some of our friends and parents in the audience. It was quite understandable in the circumstances that many have stayed away, but I'd like to extend a welcome to those that have made the effort, particularly Roy de Lisle who many of you will know, and who will have something to say I'm sure.

ROY: I'm very glad to be here and lend what support I can.

TRISH: Thank you Roy.

The lights change.

That's more like it, thank you Sarfraz. Now these sat here are all the young people who were going to be in the play. Those of you who were at the dress rehearsal yesterday… (*The visitors.*) …will know that things went a bit pear-shaped, and that our leading actor experienced a few difficulties, which basically means…

KYLIE: He walked out.

TRISH: Yes, thank you Kylie…that he is indisposed…

KYLIE: And he's not coming back.

TRISH: We don't know that yet. And we've had to turn tonight into a discussion type of thing. I want to say you're all of you welcome to ask questions, but for the moment I'm going to hand over to Bella…she's our director is Bella.

BELLA: Thank you.

AFTAB and WENDY are talking to each other.

Shut up. (*To audience.*)You probably know we decided to look at mixed relationships in Burnley as the basis of our new play. In the normal course of events, we'd have watched the play, and had a question and answer session after. As we can't do that, the next best thing has been getting along the couple the young people met for their research. This is Bilal and Catherine... I thought they could kick things off by answering questions on how they got together, if they've had any problems...and then I thought we could open it up as a general discussion, 'cos I know there's some of you who've had reservations about the whole subject, even within 'Street YY'...and then we'll... Jen has set up food in the kitchen area...

JEN: And there's strawberries and cream, so...

BELLA: Is that alright?

BILAL: I hope you're not expecting anything too brilliant...

CATHERINE: We'll do our best.

BELLA: Who'd like to set the ball rolling?

Silence.

TRISH: Who'd like to ask the first question?

Silence.

WENDY puts her hand up.

KYLIE: Typical.

TRISH: Yes, Wendy.

WENDY: Did you ever find your cat?

BILAL: No, we didn't. I should explain...this was Ole, our cat, named after Ole Gunnar Solksjaer, the Manchester United player...when the cast came to see us we'd just lost him...the trouble was he was a very friendly cat...he'd just go up to anybody on the street, and I think someone just took him...

CATHERINE: We've not seen him since.

Silence.

TRISH: Let's have another question then.

JEN: Obvious one, but that's me all over. How did you two meet?

CATHERINE: It was Tania's wasn't it?

BILAL: Tania's house.

CATHERINE: I was making a DVD about issues that affect young people; the kids wanted this particular music…

BILAL: It was the *Knight Rider* theme with Bhangra music mixed in…

CATHERINE: I asked his elder brother, and he said you should talk to my younger brother.

BILAL: I got home from work about ten o'clock at night, and my brother sent me round to Tania's house with the music…

CATHERINE: And part of my work was an audit of skills in the community, and you agreed didn't you / to come and give an interview.

BILAL: Yes, to come and give an interview.

CATHERINE: And then I persuaded you to come on a course about conflict resolution…

BILAL: A three-day course…

CATHERINE: Six-day course…

BILAL: Six-day / course.

CATHERINE: Five-day course actually.

BILAL: Five-day course. I was interested in the course, but I was more interested in Cath. After that we spent a lot more time together…she showed me all her travel photographs…

CATHERINE: Chimpanzees in the Congo…

BILAL: This was July, and I was due to fly to Singapore in August to work for Singapore Airlines. I was twenty-three…my parents were starting to talk about the possibility of me getting married, and I should start to think who it should be…as long as it was within the same caste. There was never even…never even…

CATHERINE: At that point…

BILAL: A discussion, was there?

CATHERINE: We'd had conversations about interests in life, but nothing more really because it couldn't end up being something positive.

BILAL: My father was always asking, 'Will it be soon? Will it be this year?' And I would say 'Inshallah… God willing.' The main reason I went to Malaya was to put off the pressure; though while I was in Singapore, my parents came out and we went to Karachi and met all the families and daughters who would be considered suitable for me to marry, so I didn't get away from it.

WENDY: Did you like any of them?

KYLIE: Did you like any of them?

WENDY: What's wrong with that?

KYLIE: Too many questions, dickhead.

TRISH: Kylie.

BILAL: If I'm honest, there was only one person I was thinking about, but I didn't see how it could go anywhere. Then while I was in Singapore two things happened; we made our feelings known to each other, and you told me…

CATHERINE: I was considering converting to Islam. Ever since I'd been in Burnley it was something I was interested in. It was nothing to do with Bilal at that stage.

TRISH: What was your religion before, if you don't mind my asking?

CATHERINE: I was bought up as an atheist. Mum was killed in a car crash. Dad reacted very badly to that. I'd reached the point where I was searching for a spiritual dimension to my life.

BILAL: If Cath was considering this, it meant the situation went from being impossible to having a possibility, however remote.

CATHERINE: While he was in Singapore, I set up a small community organisation, which I would need help with...

BILAL: Which meant I had a job to come back to. But as soon as I got home, I needed to get away again, because the pressure now was much more intense for me to get married, which is when we had the idea of doing some /voluntary work in Thailand...

CATHERINE: / Voluntary work in Thailand.

BILAL: A year after the Tsunami...we were working in some of the worst devastation.

CATHERINE: We took days off in the hills, and we tested each other quite a lot...

BILAL: It was a chance to see what it might be like...

CATHERINE: The / difficulties...

BILAL: Hypothetical. If we / were going...

CATHERINE: What we would face / if we decided...

BILAL: To make/ a serious effort...

CATHERINE: To get together.

BILAL: What that/ would mean.

CATHERINE: It was mostly you...

BILAL: I'ld ask all the questions...interrogate you / about your past...

CATHERINE: Prodding, poking...a lot of / questions...

BILAL: Your opinion on alcohol, drugs, past relationships...

CATHERINE: A lot of testing me on alcohol. My father's an alcoholic and I drink. And Bilal was prodding away, 'Why do you drink?' And you were forever asking me, 'Will you marry me?' There we were in Thailand, having lemon pancakes...

BILAL: Which we had every day for / breakfast...

CATHERINE: Breakfast time... 'Why do you drink? Will you marry me?' 'Anything to shut you up...yes.'

BILAL: It was mostly in the evenings. We would try and catch the sunset, sitting by the sea, having a brew, feeling the breeze on our faces... 'Will you marry me?'

CATHERINE: 'You know it will never happen.'

BILAL: 'Yes, I know it will never happen, but will you marry me?'

CATHERINE: 'Thailand will be the time we have together. You'll come back to Burnley, and get married to someone else.'

BILAL: When I got back I realised I couldn't marry anyone else. In the end, it led to my mother's brother, Uncle Hassan coming over from Karachi.

CATHERINE: He came to visit me with Bilal's mother...

BILAL: And with my kid brother to act as interpreter.

CATHERINE: I still had my cat then... Ole...whenever Uncle Hassan said anything Ole looked at him adoringly...and Uncle Hassan said it was good that I had a cat because the Prophet Mohammed, peace be upon him, liked cats, especially for their sense of independence, and it broke the ice.

WENDY puts her hand up.

CATHERINE: Yes?

WENDY: What did your dad think of you marrying an Asian?

TAMSIN: And a Muslim?

85

BILAL: Shall I answer that? I asked him one day if he would give his consent, and he said, 'She can marry an orang-utan for all I care.'

TAMSIN: Did he really say that?

CATHERINE: It wasn't meant cynically or unkindly…

BILAL: And I said, 'I can take that as a "yes" then?'

CATHERINE: It doesn't even register on the radar screen with my family. If I turned up in Ballymena in a hijab, it might get a 'What is she at now? She's always doing something weird.'

KYLIE's mobile goes. KYLIE answers it and starts to leave.

KYLIE: Oh hiya…hang on…

TRISH: Can't it wait, Kylie?

KYLIE: It's mi phone. It's really important. I'll go outside. (*To SARFRAZ and AFTAB.*) Rhode Island Coffee Shop.

AFTAB: No!

KYLIE: Told ya.

KYLIE goes outside.

AFTAB: How does she do it?

UDAY: What's this about?

AFTAB: Tell you later.

SARFRAZ: Too easy, man.

TRISH: Sorry about that. How did it go, the meeting?

CATHERINE: His mum was concerned… 'Would we visit regularly? Would I become part of their family?' I said my mum had died when I was little… I was looking forward to being part of a potential family. Uncle Hassan said 'It's not just this family that is your family now, it's everyone in Karachi.' And they left.

BILAL: Uncle Hassan went to my father and said, 'It's good, it's encouraging, it's progressive. Why delay the inevitable?'

CATHERINE: Then it was taken out of our hands, and a different sort of all hell broke loose.

BILAL: My father said, 'Right...it should all be done before Uncle Hassan goes back to Karachi...you're getting married next Thursday at six o'clock.'

CATHERINE: Which meant I converted to Islam at the same time.

KYLIE comes back in. She gives the thumbs up to AFTAB, and SARFRAZ.

KYLIE: Get in!

AFTAB: When?

KYLIE: Tomorrow.

SARFRAZ: Easy, just too easy.

TRISH: Can you take a seat quickly Kylie.

BILAL: After the ceremony, we moved in together...we sat on the sofa giggling like thirteen-year-olds...

CATHERINE: The first month I felt I was being really, really naughty. Everything I did with him, I thought, 'I shouldn't be doing this.'

BILAL: Prior to getting married, there were always official reasons for our being together. If we went anywhere, we'd go with a brother, a sister, or it would be work-related stuff.

CATHERINE: And here we were legitimately on our own. I was quite scared someone would turn up and we would be in trouble. Only we were...in trouble I mean...and it didn't take long to find out. When we were getting married we had to be secretive because of Bilal's family. But my professional colleagues thought it was their business to know what I was up to...'cos we worked in Community Cohesion, and we talk about transparency...

BILAL: It's their business to know if you're going to cross a barrier. And there were all these snide remarks as to how I'd married my boss…

CATHERINE: Nothing to do with ability. I'd given him a hand up the ladder.

BILAL: I had taken a short cut, and I was / Asian.

CATHERINE: Oh yes, he was Asian.

BILAL: Though all the Community Cohesion workers here feel the need for Asians to be embedded into the wider community…

CATHERINE: It's the Holy Grail…it creates fantastic opportunities for the liberal white do-gooders.

ROY: Oh dear…

TRISH: Yes Roy?

ROY: I have to say, 'cos I see we have outsiders here, and I don't want them to get the wrong impression…this is making it sound as if we're forever fighting amongst ourselves, which is not the case. We are all on the same side.

CATHERINE: Meant to be.

TRISH: Perhaps we should…

ROY: We're all here to do the work.

TRISH: What about another question?

CATHERINE: No you're not. That's my whole point. People are so intent on being competitive and possessive, the work doesn't get done. 'As long as you don't do better than me in Community Cohesion you're fine.'

ROY: I have to say that's nonsense, but perhaps the best thing is to let you finish and then I'll come back if I may.

TRISH: I think we might all want to say something about that.

CATHERINE: Ever since the wedding, I'm treated like an enemy, by them subtly having a go at the things I do professionally.

BILAL: We have an expression for it… 'Mitti Choori'…it means 'sweet knife'. They're polite to your face, but as soon as you turn round, they slip the blade in between the ribs.

CATHERINE: For example… GAP…my grooming project.

ROY: No. Excuse me but no.

CATHERINE: Sorry, did you say something?

ROY: I said, 'no'.

TRISH: I think what Roy's saying…

CATHERINE: What do you mean, 'no'?

ROY: Not the time, not the place.

TRISH: What he's saying is he's not sure / it's the right time…

CATHERINE: What are you talking about, Roy?

ROY: Look around you. We've got outsiders here, we've got young people here…this is not the time or place to be discussing these sort of issues.

CATHERINE: Why not?

ROY: This is an issue we know about in Social Services…it's being dealt with…and it's not a story that should be put into the public domain.

CATHERINE: Why?

ROY: Because…

CATHERINE: It's not your issue to own…it's already in the public domain.

ROY: Because…

CATHERINE: It's not even a Burnley issue, it's a national issue. It's not yours to own.

BILAL: Burnley…Burnley…you can't see anything beyond Burnley.

BELLA: Actually I have to say… I think there's a lot of issues which are being swept under the carpet.

TRISH: Perhaps if we…

BELLA: People are forever saying, 'This shouldn't be brought out into the open', 'That shouldn't be'. There's a real culture of secrecy here…we have all these meetings, say a 'Conflict Resolution' meeting, and then the results are kept under wraps…always under the pretext 'What if this information gets into the wrong hands?' I think secrecy causes myth, and myth causes problems, so yes, I think this is something we should be discussing.

TRISH: Perhaps if we let Catherine put her point, Roy, and then you can come back. And we should ask our young people. Is this something we should be discussing or is it best left? Is that alright?

ROY: Alright, but you should think very seriously about who's here and what's suitable.

TRISH: We'll certainly bear that in mind. Yes Wendy?

WENDY: The plays 'Street YY' put on are about problems young people face. What's grooming if it isn't a problem young people have to deal with?

KYLIE: Like being a lezzer.

BELLA: / Not now Kylie.

TRISH: Not now Kylie. Does anyone disagree with that?

TAMSIN: I liked the point about…

TRISH: Yes Tamsin…

TAMSIN: It's not just Burnley. This goes on all over.

TRISH: I think what Roy's saying, and it's a very good point, is that 'cos of The Disturbances and the unemployment and what have you, you've only to mention the word Burnley,

and things what wouldn't normally hit the headlines
in another town, 'cos it's here get blown up out of all
proportion.

ROY: Thank you Trish.

TAMSIN: But we still need to have an informed opinion. And
you can't have an informed opinion if it's kept under
wraps.

CATHERINE: Which is why I've been doing a lot of work
in trying to raise awareness in this town…and I've met
resistance all the way.

ROY: Not resistance. For the reasons Trish mentioned, we do
have to be very diplomatic. And there's the racial issues as
well.

TRISH: Yes, well maybe it's time / to move on.

CATHERINE: Here we go.

BILAL: I knew it wouldn't be long before race came up.

CATHERINE: If you're not familiar with it, 'Grooming' is when
older men / treat young girls…

TRISH: You know Catherine…this / might not be the best
time…

CATHERINE: No, sorry…when older men treat young girls…

BILAL: Here it's mostly white girls and older Asian men…
that's why he says 'racial issues'.

BELLA: White men as well…

BILAL: Oh yes…and that's an important point…it's a social
issue, not a racial issue.

ROY: But it would be perceived as being a racial issue, and we
have to take that into account.

BELLA: There you go again. How something is perceived is
more important than how it actually is.

ROY: It has to be taken into account, yes.

CATHERINE: They buy these young girls presents, drinks, take them out to dinner, make them feel special…

BILAL: And then exploit them for sex…quite often underage girls…fourteen, thirteen even.

CATHERINE: Not just for themselves, but for their friends, their relatives. With a group of volunteers, I applied for funding on County level to start an awareness programme going. There seemed to be a gap in our understanding, and a gap in our response, so we christened the whole thing GAP… Grooming Awareness Project. We submitted a comprehensive and progressive agenda, and it met with approval. We were told funding was on its way.

BILAL: That funding caused an uproar…

ROY: (*Private.*) You see Trish… I told you…

TRISH: (*Private.*) I'm not sure / I can do anything to stop her.

CATHERINE: Burnley's budget for projects allied to Community Cohesion was increased from fifty thousand to seventy-five thousand, with twenty-five thousand specifically earmarked for the GAP / programme.

BILAL: Had it been Joe Bloggs who got the money, there would have been / no issue.

CATHERINE: I've only been in Burnley a comparatively short time. I was seen to be treading on a lot / of toes…

BILAL: Lot of / jealousy…

CATHERINE: And there's still an attitude to women pioneering the work, so it's all about professional jealousy. And you can't get away from it…you've blocked our funding.

ROY: It irks me to say this to you publicly, but you're talking nonsense.

CATHERINE: Then where's the money?

ROY: It's not being blocked. It's being processed. At the moment we're co-ordinating the various strands to see how the problem can be /tackled most effectively.

CATHERINE: In other words you've blocked it. That money was allocated to GAP.

ROY: Excuse me… If you'll just let me finish…tackled most effectively. For two reasons…firstly it would be irresponsible for me in my position to release the money without ensuring that the proper monitoring structures are in place; that's standard practice; and secondly, to merge this new scheme into the larger picture. We all need to be grouped under the one umbrella. For all your meteoric rise, I'm still your senior, and it's my decision what we do about this problem, and when.

CATHERINE: Which, as far as I can see, means doing nothing.

ROY: Far from it, but as Trish has already pointed out…this could be the next big thing. You know what the media are like…as soon as a place gets a reputation for negative stories, they sit around like vultures waiting for any bit of bad news and suddenly it's tabloid headlines, and everyone says 'Oh here we go… Burnley again.' Why should anywhere…especially a town that's trying to recover from a rocky time, have to be tarnished with the actions of a few irresponsible individuals? It's just not a true representation of the place. And it knocks us back to square one.

BELLA: On the other hand, if you keep it quiet, it looks as if you're condoning it.

TAMSIN: I go along with that.

ROY: So what we've learned, what we've had to learn, is to tread very carefully…which is what we're doing…dealing with the problems without creating a fuss.

BELLA: Fine, except as far as I can tell, you're not really dealing with anything. If you go out my house and turn left, onto Coverdale Road, I see it all the time…men in cars chatting up young girls and then whisking them off into the sunset.

TAMSIN: Not just Coverdale Road. Try outside The Paradise on a Friday night.

BELLA: I see a lot of work being done by us lot on the ground, but at the higher level nothing's being done at all.

TRISH: Bella…

BELLA: Sorry, sorry, but it makes me angry. It happens all the time here…there is an issue, there are things in place to deal with that issue, but something gets stuck at a crucial level.

ROY: Not stuck, moving with caution.

CATHERINE: I've got a case at the moment…not fourteen or thirteen…this is an eleven year-old girl…

WENDY: Eleven…

CATHERINE: Being passed from a taxi driver to a businessman to a…

ROY: Enough. You really shouldn't discuss this here.

CATHERINE: Don't you dare speak to me like that. I can use my own discretion. We were invited here for an open discussion.

ROY: We know about this case. It's being dealt with.

CATHERINE: What are you talking about? It's only just come to light. You don't know anything about it.

ROY: This is exactly the sort of thing I'm talking about. These things are much better discussed calmly and rationally out of the public spotlight, so that we can act in a co-ordinated fashion.

CATHERINE: You can't stand it, can you, because we've got a clearly marked strategy and it looks as if we might actually get somewhere.

ROY: We have to speak with one voice.

CATHERINE: And at the moment we're speaking with no voice at all.

TRISH: If we could all try to keep calm.

ROY: It's all very well for you. You can afford to spout all this liberal rubbish. If only you could see it from the real perspective, you'd know that we're walking in a minefield. One false step…you trigger something off.

CATHERINE: So you end up…

ROY: Will you let me finish, please. You've had your say. It's taken seven years, seven long years, to get the situation here under control. And what we've learned is you have to be very diplomatic. And what happens? In you come like a bull in a china shop, and I'm telling you…you could easily awaken all the old tensions. That's not a responsible way to behave.

CATHERINE: Are you saying I'm not responsible?

ROY: I am. And what's more I think you're selfish because you're more interested in promoting your pet theory than in maintaining a stable community.

CATHERINE: Look at the facts Roy. I've done more good in two years than you've done in twenty. And you don't listen.

ROY: You're the one who doesn't listen. It's all me, me, me, and that's why you're in danger of opening up all the old wounds.

CATHERINE: And you just paper over the cracks and run off home with a fat salary having achieved fuck all.

ROY: How dare you…

TAMSIN: Can I just say something?

TRISH: Tamsin.

TAMSIN: I was groomed in a way…Jari was that charming to start with…but at least we were the same age.

TRISH: Right.

TAMSIN: My kid sister…

TRISH: Rachel?

TAMSIN: No, she's the middle one. Jodie I'm talking about.
Jodie...she was fourteen...looking and acting about
eighteen like you do...she started disappearing on
Saturdays...tells mum and dad she's been on the bus
to Manchester to go to the shops, which was true in a
way...then it's the whole weekend...then she doesn't
come back for weeks. The odd phone call... 'I'm fine bla
bla bla...staying with friends.' Next we hear is from social
services in Chorlton...she's in rehab with a cocaine habit.
But that's not the half of it. I'll not tell you his name, but
this Bangladeshi businessman was picking her up by a
bus-stop...taking her to Manchester in his BMW, taking
her shopping, slinky red dresses, ear-rings, the lot...she's
swept off her feet...until he gave her a habit...skunk and
cocaine...housed her with his cousin...so she was there for
them whenever they wanted, and the other uncle, and his
friend. What she told me was she was that desperate for
the cocaine, they took her clothes off, put the cocaine in
a saucer on the floor and said, 'Come on little pussy' and
when she went down to snort it up, they took her from
behind...until she crawled out the window one night. And
now she doesn't look eighteen, she looks about thirty-five.
So yes, I think this is a story people should know about.
People should be aware of what's going on on their own
doorstep, but I can quite see for a town that's had a bad
time, it's not the sort of story they want to be associated
with.

TRISH: Oh this is awful, awful.

ROY: I'm sorry about your sister, I truly am...and I'm sure the
appropriate action will be taken...but you see...all these
stories...they're all negative stories, negative, negative,
negative...all they do is give people the idea this is the
worst racist place in the country. I happen to think there's a
lot going for this place.

BELLA: Oh yes. 'Look at the lovely hills, the rolling moors,
the rippling streams.' But if you dare to speak out, if you

dare tell a story like that, all you get is, 'It'll put people off bringing new investment to the town.'

ROY: But it's true. We're desperate for new investment… new jobs; none of you seem to understand how careful we have to be about our image to the outside world.

BELLA: Sell your soul to the devil you mean.

TRISH: Bella.

JEN: And the other thing of course, if you say things as they really are, you're told to 'keep your gob shut 'cos it's food and drink for the BNP', and that's the excuse they use for everything.

ROY: Again, again…it's true…all you do by concentrating on the negative is hand the political advantage to the BNP.

BELLA: How many times have we heard this? 'We don't want the BNP getting hold of this, 'cos it'll appear on their next leaflet.' And it will, course it will; we're not born yesterday, we know the score. Tell me this, Roy…why should the BNP dictate the way we run our town?

ROY: Because they'll use anything and everything to stir up racial tension.

BELLA: All the more reason to stand up to them. We all know they're clever at manipulation…stoking people up into this false nostalgia for the past…

WENDY: My mum's like that. She voted BNP.

JEN: You've only to listen to 'em for five minutes…it's all, 'Do you remember how it were golden age?'

WENDY: On and on about how she misses the old days.

JEN: 'Didn't have much money, but it were golden age. Knew everyone in street…leave your back door open…ask your neighbour for a cup of sugar.'

WENDY: 'Only had one broom between four families…always round mi Auntie Marjory's asking for broom.' Sounds shit to me.

JEN: They see emptiness and bleak lives where there used to be something. It's got to be somebody's fault…might as well blame the Asians…if they weren't here, it would be someone else. It's all about a sense of loss and disappointment, and that's an easy thing to tap into.

BELLA: So don't tell us not to look at the issues because of the BNP; otherwise the issues never get dealt with.

ROY: They do get dealt with, but not in such a way as it's in your face the whole time.

ANEESA: Listening to you lot…

TRISH: Yes, Aneesa, have you got something you want to say?

ANEESA: Listening to you lot, do you know what strikes me?

TRISH: You'd better tell us.

ANEESA: It's OTT…everything's OTT nowadays. All the problems are blown up out of all proportion, so somebody can deal with them.

ROY: What do you mean exactly?

ANEESA: I mean exactly that. Any problem which comes along and could be dealt with relatively easily, is chewed over and mauled about until it becomes this huge grotesque thing that everyone has to be concerned about. I'm not taking a holier-than-thou position… I catch miself doing it all the time.

ROY: I don't know how to reply to that, except to say it's a very cynical point of view. If you had spent as much time working here as I have, you would know that these problems exist. We're not making them worse, we're not exaggerating them…they just are.

ANEESA: Not really, not if you think about it; what else is there to do? There's hardly any proper jobs in Burnley; no industry to speak of…very little service industry…the shopping's crap…there's not a single decent hotel…the transport's shit…so what are we left with? Problems.

Problems are our biggest industry. There's more community workers here than anything else. Which is why any little thing that comes along, however trivial, is blown up into an issue, so we can all justify our existence.

ROY: Again you're speaking without any real knowledge of what's been allowed to happen since the industry collapsed; and the infrastructure collapsed, along with the lack of government understanding; and, by the way, I hope you're not saying what we've heard tonight was trivial.

ANEESA: There you go...no doubt you'll want to blow all this up into an issue, and it'll come up at some meeting or other...and there'll be another load of infighting...and scalps will be demanded...and it'll end up as yet another example of how you never get to the core of anything, 'cos you're always arguing over who's going to do something and how, rather than trying to address the problem itself.

ROY: You talk as if there were overnight solutions. This is the sort of work that takes time.

ANEESA: We'd get there a damn sight quicker if we weren't all constantly undermining each other and stabbing each other in the back.

ROY: I repeat...it takes a long time to build up trust.

TRISH: I think we'd all agree with that.

ROY: I think you're demeaning the commitment of the people in Burnley, who are doing important work.

ANEESA: Who says it's important?

ROY: I do.

ANEESA: Exactly what I'm saying. It has to be 'important', so you can give it your expert attention. Have you ever seen yourself? I'm sorry Roy, but it's like you're always trying to be involved and concerned...concerned with a capital 'C'. If there's a group of white and a group of Asian in a room, as often as not you'll go up to the Asian group first, and say, 'You're so welcome', smiling serenely…it's all faked, it's all forced… and shoving a samosa down your throat.

SARFRAZ: Motherfucker.

ROY: (*Getting up.*) That's it…

TRISH: I'm sure she didn't mean / it like that.

ANEESA: We wouldn't be there in the first place if we weren't comfortable with the situation. I'm British Asian… I have an identity. I don't need to be protected from the BNP I don't need to be patronised. Least of all to be patronised by you, and told what I can and can't discuss.

ROY: I'm sorry; the record has to be put straight here. We've made a lot of headway in this town.

ANEESA: When you say 'we' are you including me? 'Cos I certainly haven't. And as far as I can see neither have you. You've not fixed the unemployment; you've not fixed the low aspirations; you've not fixed the drug-taking, you've not fixed the grooming. All you do, all any of us can do is pick the scabs, and play nurse when they start to bleed.

ROY: That's outrageous and demeaning.

ANEESA: But it's true.

ROY: You've no right…listen…we've dedicated our lives to the problems here with a great deal of compassion; a real belief that we can do something to improve the long-term lives of the people, specially the young people. And if you don't believe that, then I'm sorry, but you're a sad person. (*To us.*) I don't know who you are, but I hope you'll behave responsibly with the material you've seen and heard. Because this, what you've heard here…this cynical and pessimistic rubbish…it's not a true representation of Burnley…nothing like. This is why I get fed up with you lot coming here and stirring things up; the wrong sort of people get hold of it and make political capital out of it, and we're still dealing with it long after you've left. Whether you mean to or not, you could drag this town right back to where it was in 2001. And another thing…what you don't realise is that Youth Work is only a hairsbreadth away from being axed altogether…there's already one town round here that's lost its funding…and I want to do everything in my power to make sure we're not the next one.

Do you know what I feel? I feel my professionalism has been called into question here this evening, and my commitment…and I'll not have that…not at any price.

TRISH: Roy…

ROY: No…that's my last word. Goodnight.

ROY goes.

TRISH: Goodnight. Right. Right. You see the difficulties we face. Shall we get back to the…has anyone else got a question for Catherine and Bilal?

CATHERINE: No, I'm sorry. I think we should go as well. This isn't what I had in mind… I never meant it to turn acrimonious either.

BILAL: I think we've / probably overstepped the mark.

CATHERINE: We've overstayed our welcome.

TRISH: No, no…you've brought up a lot of…

CATHERINE: It's alright. You don't have to make excuses for us. It's best if we go. If I'm honest I don't think we'll be here much longer.

TRISH: What do you mean?

CATHERINE: In Burnley.

BILAL: We've got to the point where / we're thinking of leaving Burnley.

CATHERINE: I've a feeling I'll never get GAP off the ground here 'cos of all the infighting. I'm prepared to give it a month, and then…

BILAL: Time to go.

CATHERINE: So thanks…

BILAL: Yes, thanks, and I'm sorry if it all got out of control.

BELLA: Not a bit if it. Thank you for coming.

ALL: Yes, thanks for coming.

CATHERINE: OK, 'bye everybody.

CATHERINE and BILAL go.

TRISH: Right…not quite what we had in mind…but…right, has anybody else got something they want to say before we go and have something to eat?

ANEESA: I've not finished.

TRISH: Right. Sorry, you've got more you want to say Aneesa?

ANEESA: Yes, I have as it turns out…seeing as it's come up. I don't know what anyone else thinks, but it's very interesting, in't it…what you're allowed to say and what you aren't?

TRISH: In what way?

ANEESA: What is allowed to be aired publicly, and what has to kept under wraps for the general good, or what is perceived to be the general good.

TRISH: I think Roy's in a very difficult position.

ANEESA: I wasn't necessarily talking about Roy. What about this group? Are we in a difficult position?

TRISH: Why do you ask that?

ANEESA: What are we allowed to say about this group? 'Cos it's always 'what wonderful work we do' and 'how progressive we are', and nobody seems to question the direction we're going in, and I'm not always sure…

TRISH: Yes?

ANEESA: I don't see it as being all that wonderful or progressive.

TRISH: Right. Do you want to elaborate?

ANEESA: 'Oh look at all these wonderful mixed relationships…'…as if crossing the line is the be-all and end-all…something we should all be aiming for.

UDAY: I've been questioning this.

ANEESA: But what I'm asking is, 'How many plays have you written in praise of Asian culture? How many plays have you written that show how good and progressive arranged marriages can be?'

UDAY: I'd second that.

BELLA: Like yours, you mean?

ANEESA: What are you saying?

BELLA: You know what I'm saying.

ANEESA: I've had a very positive experience.

BELLA: Say that again, so I can pinch myself. You've had a what?

ANEESA: I've had mi difficulties, but as a learning curve, it's been a progressive situation.

BELLA: You know, right now my head could spin off with anger. I don't know if you remember one night when we were on a residential…

ANEESA: Course I do.

BELLA: You couldn't stop crying.

ANEESA: That was then; this is now.

BELLA: And what happened when you got to Pakistan…

ANEESA: Yes, I know what you're going to say…

BELLA: We heard you went on hunger strike. You virtually disappeared for two years. We were worried sick.

TRISH: We were all worried actually.

BELLA: If I'm being honest, you're not the person you were.

ANEESA: What do you mean by that?

BELLA: When I see you now…always the long face. Where's that person you were when we first met?

ANEESA: I was a girl. Now I'm older and wiser.

BELLA: Where's the spark?

ANEESA: The spark?

BELLA: We had fun…the way you used to laugh all the time. You know you did…perhaps I've said too much, but I'm sorry Aneesa…

ANEESA: Yes, I know, I know…oh shit, oh shit… (*Breakdown.*) …why do I always do this to myself?

TRISH: This is going from bad to worse.

BELLA: I'm sorry, but I couldn't just sit there.

WENDY: Why's she so upset?

TRISH: Would you like a brew?

UDAY: Answer to everything.

JEN: I'll do it. (*Goes.*)

AFTAB: Can we have a game of Fußball now?

TRISH: Just stay there will you.

AFTAB: Alright, alright. I thought we'd finished.

ANEESA: It's my fault. Why did I have to open mi big fat gob? I've messed up the whole evening.

TRISH: I shouldn't worry. The evening was well shot to pieces already.

UDAY: She has got a point.

TRISH: I think we could leave the subject now…

UDAY: No. I'm sorry Trish, but no. I've been saying this all along. You can't just do a play to someone and expect them to go off and have a relationship with someone of a different race or a different background as if it's something you should be doing. You have to respect tradition.

TAMSIN: Catherine and Bilal have done that, haven't they?

UDAY: I'm not saying they haven't, but Aneesa's right… there's still this idea, even within this group, that to have an arranged marriage is backwards.

WENDY: That's not true. All we're saying is people should be free to choose.

KYLIE: We all know why she's saying that.

WENDY: Oh go and fuck yourself.

TRISH: Language Wendy please.

KYLIE: I'm going out for a fag. (*Goes.*)

UDAY: And there's still this idea that we've all got to change… like adapt and change to a better way of life, and like tomorrow…not next month or next year…tomorrow.

AFTAB: It's not all bad that comes out of family…we do have strong family loyalties

UDAY: Yes, and it's up to people here to respect that.

WENDY: Can I ask something?

TRISH: Yes Wendy.

WENDY: What happened in Pakistan? Did you really go on hunger strike?

TRISH: I'm not sure that's an entirely appropriate question. Not just at the moment.

WENDY: So this is something else we're not allowed to know what's going on?

TRISH: I would say, and I don't want to presume anything, but I would say what we were discussing before…whether it was right or wrong…was broadly speaking political…and this what Aneesa's alluded to is personal…so it's different territory.

ANEESA: You've started speaking as if I'm not in the room.

TRISH: And another concern, if you don't mind my pointing it out…we're not alone.

ANEESA: I don't mind speaking in front of strangers…it's you lot I'm worried about. But I think you should know what happened. It might help you understand…all of you actually. I was in the last year of doing mi degree at Uni…

WENDY: Is this it?

AFTAB: Sh!

WENDY: Sorry.

ANEESA: And yes I was young and fun-loving…and one of mi friends studied at Reading Uni, and she came to visit me, and bought these two Asian guys with her, and one of them had taken a blue Wkd bottle out of his bag, and I said, 'Can you put that away please? I share my flat with people who practise Islam, and I won't have alcohol in one of my cups.' And then he wouldn't listen, and within ten minutes I chucked them both out, and this guy said, 'Don't change yourself… I like your attitude.'

OK, move on. We met a few times after that, and my friends constantly teased me 'cos they said he came out the car like he'd gelled his hair, dressed up like he was out on the pull. I met this guy a maximum of six times… I didn't have physical contact of any sort…although one time it was over a period of six days. He took me out…he was the perfect gentleman…looking across the table at me with his big brown eyes… I wanted to melt into his arms…

JEN: (*From the side.*) Do you take milk and sugar?

ANEESA: Just milk thank you.

JEN: Slice o'cake? Coffee and walnut, or lemon drizzle?

ANEESA: I'm fine, really. Cup o' tea…great.

JEN: Comin' up. (*Goes.*)

ANEESA: However…however…he was six years older than me, married, not divorced, but sort of separated, and with a child. After Uni I continued talking to him on the phone… I liked him a lot… I wanted to marry him… I was on the phone to him all night.

WENDY: Did you pay or him?

ANEESA: He did. Mum would come into mi bedroom at ten in the morning and I wouldn't have slept. I told mi mum… she told mi dad…not because she's Asian and oppressed, but because she realises your dad's not going to think of anything bad for you for one second.

JEN comes back in with a cup of tea.

JEN: I've bought you a slice of cake an' all.

ANEESA: You're being very kind.

JEN: Just leave it if you don't want it.

ANEESA: Mi dad sat me down, very civilised…he obviously thought I'd had physical contact; even if I'd kissed this bloke, mi dad would have thought that was really really bad. He said, 'How do I know you haven't?' And I said, 'I'm your daughter, you'll just have to trust me on that,' and he said, he just said, 'I've got a marriage proposal for you from Pakistan, and I think you will be suited to this guy…but you have a choice… I'll cancel the engagement and let you marry this guy in Reading but I'll disown you.' He didn't actually say 'disown', but he said, 'Don't think you'll ever see your family again.'

I went back up to mi bedroom. It was ninteenth February 2005, just before ten o'clock at night…and I texted the man in Reading…stupid mobile phones… I wish no-one had ever invented them… I texted him… 'It can't happen. I'm sorry. They're about to cart me off to Pakistan. Goodbye.' If I had that decision again, I would have gone to Reading. You don't know what you've got 'til you've lost it.

Sure enough, mi parents got me engaged. It was April twelfth 2005. The weather was shit. Everyone came round to the house to congratulate me; mi dad was over the moon, and inside mi head I was saying, 'What do you know? What do any of you know of what's going on inside mi head?'

BELLA: I remember you sitting up 'til three in the morning crying... 'What shall I do? I don't know what to do.' You can't deny it.

ANEESA: I just felt defeated. I got married on August fourth. If you look at the photographs of the wedding, I look as if someone just passed away. I was very distanced from mi husband for a start; he knew something was wrong. I was taking sips of water but I wasn't eating. I just didn't want to eat. In the space of two months I had lost three stone. And then I went back to my parents' house, the one in Pakistan, and just... I was so ill they had to carry me to the bathroom. I was very, very weak by this time. They laid me on a bed...and I just remember looking up... I was in so much agony because of my weakness...that's when I looked up and prayed to the one above... 'Just make me better and I will try with my husband, I will try...' And then I told him everything, and he was very understanding, and he sat there for hours holding mi hand and spooning soup into mi gob and gradually we got to know each other, which was a scary experience to start with, but we found a way of making our marriage work. I came back in October without him. I texted the guy in Reading, and that was like, 'Oh shit, oh shit, back to square one.' And we fell into the trap of talking again, and in the back of mi head was, 'I've got a husband now I shouldn't be doing this.' Didn't stop me though.

You know when you have a chapter in a book, and you don't know the ending, and you need a closure to tie all the ends together... I need a closure with this guy, and I haven't had one.

My husband came over in January 2006. He had practically no English. We found him a job in a factory... the work force is 100 per cent Asian...earning peanuts, and sending most of it back to Pakistan, and I'd only got £2,000 saved up, and I got pregnant. It's so hard for us girls from here to continue in our careers, in our normal lives, to make the best of our education...we have dreams and aspirations...and there's barriers put in front of us if we have to get married to someone from Pakistan.

BELLA: Isn't that what I was saying?

ANEESA: Yes, but when you lot lose your dreams it's about growing up, and when I lose mi dreams you see me as being forced. Do you not see that?

Your culture is based on this idea of romantic love...and you think in an arranged marriage I must be missing out on something...it's almost as if you want me to be defeated and downtrodden to prove your point...and if by any chance my marriage happens to work, it must be a fluke... it...it...

UDAY: It can't be down to culture.

ANEESA: Well I'll tell you something...my husband, he's not typical...he's not that 'You're the woman, you do everything.' We go out and I... I...and I... I love him... I do love him, and I have an eleven month-old son and he means the world to me, but if I'm honest...really, really honest with you, if I didn't have mi son, I think I would live differently...not to go back to the other bloke...it's not about that...he's back with his ex for the kid's sake anyway...no, it's me...this is about me...for once, just once, in my life I want to think about me...my dream... going out working when I want, going out to a party... something I've chosen for miself...living in a penthouse in London...anything...but I guess it's too late for any of that now.

Silence.

COLIN comes in from outside.

COLIN: Hello.

TRISH: Hello Colin.

COLIN: Good discussion? Where are Bilal and Catherine?

TRISH: They've gone…they gave us the talk…very interesting, very thought-provoking, but it all went a bit pear-shaped really. How was your day?

COLIN: Sobering.

TRISH: I thought it might be.

COLIN: I mean I can't forget all the bad things he did to me, but when you see that coffin slide between the curtains into the flames…and seeing mi mum…she chose the music… she chose 'The Rose'…it was a Russell Watson thing… seeing her snivelling into her hankie over a man who regularly beat her to a pulp, and Father Paul struggling to find one good thing to say about the man, it does put things into perspective. You realise how fucked up Terry was by the circumstances he grew up in, and that opens up a vision of us all trying to live our lives but being screwed by things beyond our control.

JEN: Sounds familiar. Can I get you a brew?

COLIN: Ta.

JEN: There's a slice o' cake sitting there.

COLIN: No, I'm full of sausage rolls, ta.

JEN: Won't be a sec.

JEN goes to the kitchen.

COLIN: Makes yer think really, doesn't it?

TRISH: 'Course. That sounds like us, don't it…you know…like 'Street YY'…'cos that's what we've been talking about… like the gloves came off, and we've been talking about our work, and if it's any good, and Uday and Aneesa seem to have doubts…let alone whether I'm fit to run it.

UDAY: Oh come on Trish, no-one's saying that...we all think the world of you...but I have to be honest. I don't think some of the plays we do have worked as a product...

TRISH: And I keep saying it's the process not the product...

UDAY: And I'm saying they haven't really worked as process either...

TRISH: Are you?

UDAY: Yes, because there aren't many Asian girls involved, and most of the Asian boys have left the group or dropped out during rehearsals. And if we don't have any Asian kids, apart from the odd one, how much of the true story can you really show?

BELLA: It's not just that we don't get enough Asian girls; we don't get enough white boys either...but if there wasn't a problem we wouldn't need the group would we? And that's the whole point...to provide a place for them to come if they want to...where they'll be welcome...and can be involved in a positive experience.

ANEESA: I may be wrong, but it strikes me you're always preaching to the converted. You haven't got along the people who could make a difference.

TRISH: I have to admit you've got a point there...that's a continuing sadness to me... (*To the audience.*) ...here you have a group of young people trying to discuss issues which could make a difference to their lives, and only one councillor from Burnley has been to any of the performances of any of the plays we have done.

JEN comes in with a cup of tea.

JEN: There you go.

COLIN: Thanks.

TAMSIN: I think for our next project we should build a play just using what people say in real life.

JEN: People like us you mean?

BELLA: Yes, it's a very good point, and most of the plays I've done have incorporated real stories... but when you say about the process... I couldn't disagree more that it hasn't been beneficial, because it absolutely has...it's done amazing things in terms of confidence building... I see it in all of you...working together on a project, affirms the positive, and it spreads into other parts of your lives.

TRISH: You have achieved something you never thought you could, and I don't want to lose sight of that, because this will have a knock-on effect. You Uday...the reason you have such a powerful voice, and can be so persuasive, is because 'Street YY' has given you that platform so to speak. I'm right, aren't I?

UDAY: Yes, I hold mi hand up, that's true, but that doesn't stop me pointing out the things we're getting wrong.

TRISH: And I wouldn't want you to stop. But that confidence you've got now...that's what we can give young lives...a belief they can achieve, and make them feel supported enough not to doubt it.

KYLIE comes back in.

TRISH: Look at you Kylie...

KYLIE: What about me?

TRISH: Look what 'Street YY' has done for you. You've got this part in a play in Manchester.

KYLIE: Everyone here's dead jealous. These people from Manchester came to see the last play we did...offered me the part just like that. We had six months to learn the lines for this play we're doing now...we've only got four weeks for the one in Manchester, and the script's that thick.

TRISH: Sarfraz is going to take over the world.

SARFRAZ: I want to open my own business, you get me. I wanna be my own chief. Somebody says to me 'Get me a pint of lager', I'll say, 'Get it yer fucking self, motherfucker, you've got legs haven't yer?' You know me... I've done everything… I started selling drugs at fourteen, but I've stopped all that. Everyone fucks up at a bad age. What's sad about Burnley is you find people fucking up at the age of forty-one.

TRISH: Wendy's another high-flyer…

WENDY: I'm going to Preston with Aftab next year, and I'm going to study psychology, sociology, anthropology…

KYLIE: Lesbiology…

BELLA: Kylie.

WENDY: And then on to university.

AFTAB: You know Wends, I only said I might.

WENDY: It's alright. I know at heart I'm only another side dish. But I can cope. I'm a big girl now. Before I came to 'Street YY', I could never stand up in front of people, but now I don't care what people think, 'cos I like myself… I do…finally.

TRISH: But these, I have to admit, are the exception. There's loads of others who could become success stories… absolutely…but there aren't enough people to spend that quality time with them to get them started. So, for every one of these here, there's five that fall through the net. There's a lot of people in this place facing a bleak future.

JEN: The trouble is it's been so long since the Town were up and running, people now feel thick and stupid. The thought of anything new coming along scares the hell out of them. I have parents saying, 'I can't even turn on a computer. I do feel thick and stupid.' You've got to give them hope.

TRISH: We do our best.

JEN: OK, but it's pissing in the wind frankly. They do have a vision for this place, but it's a vision for fifteen years' time. And I'm sure it will be better…a university, better transport, turning the mills into flats and bowling alleys.

But what about now? 'Cos what I see is all the people who have the knowledge are leaving...like you lot. What about them as can't leave? Who's doing anything for them? That's two...three generations being written off as collateral damage... Bad luck, you wre born in the wrong place at the wrong time...and people like us...all we're doing in reality's picking up the pieces that fall through gaps.

UDAY: The best work we do is always for an for an individual...trying to tell young people there's something more to life than getting smashed at ten in the morning and having sex under a bush. I know in reality it's only damage limitation.

JEN: At the back of it, cleaning up...that's what we do; that's all we can do. Go round the back cleaning up of it. I'm back to kitchen.

JEN starts to go. She sees JAVED and MAUREEN coming in.

Bloody hell, look what the wind's blown in.

BELLA: I don't believe it.

TAMSIN: Better late than never.

JAVED: I came back.

BELLA: We can see that.

JAVED: I came to say sorry.

MAUREEN: And...

BELLA: And?

MAUREEN: Tell them. Tell them what's happened.

JAVED: We're engaged.

COLIN: That were quick.

AFTAB: Bloody hell.

KYLIE: Could have told yer.

TRISH: I suppose we should say 'congratulations'.

BELLA: And do you still want to do the play?

JAVED: Is that alright?

BELLA: Alright by me.

TRISH: What does that mean?

BELLA: That means we do a dress rehearsal tomorrow afternoon; and do the play tomorrow night.

TRISH: Have you got that everybody…one o'clock tomorrow for a group warm-up, ready to go at two o'clock for a dress rehearsal.

JAVED: Maureen's got a question.

TRISH: Yes, go on Maureen.

MAUREEN: I want to be in it.

BELLA: You serious?

MAUREEN: Yes.

BELLA: Right, one o'clock tomorrow.

KYLIE: (*To MAUREEN.*) You up the duff?

MAUREEN: No. Why?

KYLIE: Why else would he want to marry an old slapper like you?

MAUREEN: Takes one to know one.

BELLA: Oy, enough.

JEN: Is everyone ready for a brew and something to eat?

TRISH: Very nice Jen. It's such a shame… I know our friends here have got to leave tomorrow morning…you'll not get to see the play.

BELLA: Well we could give them a taster…while we've got everyone here… Colin, could you do the lights and sound for the last scene?

COLIN: I could.

BELLA: Don't bother with costumes or anything like that. If you all put the chairs to one side... Sarfraz, give a hand with the chairs. Aftab, where do you stand for that last scene?

AFTAB: Here.

BELLA: And the four girls...

TAMSIN: Lined up here.

KYLIE: Mind mi fucking feet.

BELLA: Aneesa.

ANEESA: Oh mi eyes are a mess.

BELLA: You look fine.

JAVED: And me, and me...

BELLA: Oh how could I ever forget you? Uday at the side. How nearly are you ready Colin?

COLIN: Give me a couple of seconds.

BELLA: Have you got the tape lined up?

COLIN: Yes.

BELLA: We'll go from the line, 'Another week, another prize; another dream takes to the skies'.

TAMSIN: We're going from 'Another week, another surprise'.

BELLA: Is that alright?

TAMSIN: Is that alright?

TRISH: And I want to say, because you may not realise it, but the words to this song...well it's a poem really...have been written by Wendy...and it scans and everything...so I think that's quite an achievement.

COLIN: Ready.

BELLA: Right.

The music starts and the stage is flooded in orange and red light.

The company perform the walk-down number from the Rikki Rajah Show.

COMPANY: 'Another week, another prize;
               Another dream takes to the skies;
               No matter where you want to go,
               It's on the Rikki Rajah Show.

               This town was football, coal and cotton,
               But now the industry's forgotten.
               The cobbled streets that heard the sound of clipping clogs
               Are now the haunt of cats and feral dogs;
               The mills lie empty to the clouds,
               And tattered fabrics hang like shrouds
               And all the looms that made the precious yarn
               Where are they now? They're all in fucking Pakistan.
               The only thing now made in reams
               Are people's disenchanted dreams.
               But if you think we're down and out, and giving up,
               Resigned to drink and drowning in a bitter cup,
               Then think again. We'll not lie down,
               Nor stop the fight to save this town.
               There's something here to raise us up and lift the gloom,
               More powerful than any factory or loom,
               And that's the spirit of our crew,
               And when the crunch comes we'll show you,
               "It may look bleak, we're up against the wall my friend,
               But we are one, so rest assured, it's not the end."
               So join with us, and sing along
               To Rikki Rajah's song.'

The whole COMPANY joins in the final chorus.

'Another week, another prize;
Another dream takes to the skies.
No matter where you want to go,
It's on the Rikki Rajah Show.'

End.

Interview with Robin Soans

Robin Soans's previous verbatim plays include *Talking to Terrorists*, *The Arab Israeli Cookbook*, *A State Affair* – which showed life on a Bradford Council Estate – and *Life After Scandal*, about Christine and Neil Hamilton. Here he talks about the possibilities, and responsibilities, of making theatre from real people's words.

Where did the idea come from for Mixed Up North*?*

I'd been thinking of writing a play set in Coventry, about four marriages, one of which would be a mixed marriage. That project fell through and this seemed a natural successor. It seemed to encapsulate most of the themes that one would really want to write about this particular phase in history – the bleak, holocaustic element after the industrial revolution collapsed very suddenly in historical terms. You begin to see the end of it in *Rita, Sue and Bob Too*, the Andrea Dunbar play. Here we are 25 years later and I would say there's still a rather bleak landscape for many people.

It seems to me you can't write a political play. You can't write a play about all those historical moments and political things. You write a play about some people, people who are in the middle of these movements in history and you'll get that just by studying their lives and the situations in which they find themselves, and it ends up being a political play.

Did you have a fixed idea of what you wanted the play to be or did it develop from the research in Burnley?

One of my golden rules is that you don't have a fixed agenda, otherwise you start moulding the stuff you're finding into a fixed pattern. You stop being as inquisitive as you might be otherwise. It's better to go in with a completely open mind and find what's going on. It doesn't limit your research and it's always a great idea not to limit yourself immediately.

You get a multiplicity of ideas, this huge expanse of emotions and situations and you have to find a way of linking them all together. In this instance it was taking the kids through a dress rehearsal which went wrong and the aftermath of that.

The two acts of this play are both in actual time so there's no hiding: whatever happens in that hour happens in that hour, whether it be food or a meal being prepared or something going wrong. But once you've got that framework it allows you to fill that hour with nearly all the things you've found.

I had a lengthy interview with a woman from the BNP and although a little bit of what she said has leeched into other characters' lines, it seems a pity I can't fit her into the play. It was the same with the liaison officer of Burnley Football Club. Fascinating man but again it doesn't quite fit into the scheme of the play. We went to the House of Commons and interviewed Kitty Usher, the MP, and we interviewed Alistair Campbell. It's not a waste of time all this, because the more you can accrue information and different points of view about the town the better.

How objective is it?

I know it can't be objective. If you gave David Hare, David Edgar, myself and Alecky Blythe this material you would end up with four different plays. It is a mystery to me that somehow verbatim is a restrictive way of writing. I absolutely disagree. The bricks may be the same but the structure you build with them is entirely idiosyncratic and that's my vision of the world. That's what an artist does, he creates his particular vision of the material.

In many ways Mixed Up North *is a rather old-fashioned, left-wing, Marxist sort-of play – wicked capitalism and the effect it has on people.*

Burnley is the victim of economic change and the preservation of profit. In Burnley and South Wales and elsewhere, a traditional way of manufacturing came to an almost guillotine-style halt. If you look at the historical context of it – the cottage-industry of weaving in Burnley started up in the fourteenth century – it's been going for 600 years then suddenly in a decade it's all gone.

No social cushioning was put in place to soften the blow, and I would like to point out there is a social cost – a social, emotional, educational cost to be paid for the big businesses keeping their profits and not spending some of their profits in putting in social cushioning for the people whose lives have been blasted.

So I think the real villains in this play aren't in Burnley at all, I think they're in government, probably in national government and in the markets, in the big multi-national companies. Colin says it in the play – 'Someone realised…send the raw materials to Pakistan, have the labour done there by 20p a day workers, and have it shipped back…it costs you less than keeping the factories open.' Well that's fine for the person who's making millions of pounds profit a year.

Before this disappears into history, before Burnley becomes a well-healed suburb of Manchester with lovely hills to walk up and The Body Shop moves in and it becomes lots of tea shops and all the mills become bowling alleys and wedding reception centres and conference centres and flats, I think it's important just to realise there was a time when human beings behaved in a way that was less than perfect. So that if the same thing was to happen again maybe we could learn something from it.

Where do ethnic divisions fit in to this?

This is a play about racism but it's not a play about 'racism'. It's a play about a group of people, some of whom happen to be racist in one way or another – it's one of these ludicrous questions. Like George Bush saying 'you're either for us or against us'. It's a complex issue, racism. I think it's better to listen to people talking and to ask, what sort of things make those arise? Parental issues, traditional issues, issues of jealousy, issues of what people used to have and don't have anymore. And if we think that's racist, or if we can understand how that's come about, then that's more interesting than me imposing some sort of view of my own.

How did you research the play?

I've been to Burnley at least ten times. Before we started the project at LAMDA, me and a researcher, Jesse Quinones, spent three days there, just so I could see the territory and meet people.

It doesn't sound much but if you work from 9am to 11pm you can see an enormous number of people. In that time I went to an inter-faith feast and met the MP and interviewed 15 to 18 people and went to watch the theatre group do their production. So that when I started at LAMDA I had already made lots of contacts, and I knew where the gaps were – if you've got one point of view you always want to meet someone who's got an opposing point of view.

This play has given rise to an enormous number of issues as to what is and isn't acceptable and how people's lives might be perceived to be exploited, so there have been many meetings over the past year where I have tried to make people feel included and see that they have an input into the play. It's very important that we don't seem to be riding rough-shod over people's lives, and if they feel very strongly that something shouldn't be included in the play we've made compromises so it's not. It's extraordinary that this play, out of all the plays I've written, has been the most contentious.

Were you surprised by the controversy over the play?

Not really. Dignity and identity are important component parts of the human psyche. People in places like Burnley have had a really rough time because their traditional way of life has just been removed, and that does a lot of damage to the infrastructure and the confidence of the town; it puts people off bringing investment to the town. I think people are quite protective of the place because they want to feel proud of it and of who they are and I absolutely understand that.

Burnley isn't like going into Chipping Camden or Lavendum or somewhere – 'Should we have a blue sign or a pink sign, should we have pansies or wall flowers in the corporation beds?' – those rather middling problems. Of course people in those places would say young people are behaving very badly, but I think the issues in somewhere like Burnley are more severe because a whole way of life has been removed.

What do you say to people who argue you shouldn't come in as an outsider and exploit their community?

If you're trying to look at somewhere objectively it's much better to be an outsider, and to come in with a blank agenda. Especially somebody who is used to looking at situations like the Middle East, like terrorism, like heroin addiction on a Bradford estate, like people whose lives have been influenced by scandal. A liberal-minded outsider might be able to see an overall picture that you in the middle of it aren't going to be able to see. That's why when theatre directors have got a show that's about to open, very often they ask an outsider to get an objective view of it, to get a fresh pair of eyes.

Some people might say you are a liberal and that's what the problem is – you can't understand it from their perspective.

But I think if they look their perspective is put in there. I'm trying to open up that debate and say well actually there is actually rather more to this than meets the eye, come and look at the play and I might be able to make you at least question your point of view by showing the currents that make people behave how they behave. That's what I'm trying to do in many ways and for any audience.

It isn't a grim play – there's a difference between being grim and being serious, this play's very serious but here's a great deal of humour in it. At the same time as trying to show people the complexity of a situation, you're trying to entertain them. There's not much point in getting 300 people in a darkened room if you're going to bore them rigid.

Some of the students from the youth club in Burnley came to see the show in LAMDA. What did they think of it?

They were really overjoyed by it, they had a really uplifting evening, because it was relevant. I think there's a great fear that there's something very worthy about going to the theatre and they're going to have to sort of battle through it and have a nice drink afterwards and feel worthy for having gone to the theatre. I don't really like writing plays like that.

You've worked with Max Stafford-Clark several times. What do you think it is about this working relationship that's been so successful?

We're both liberal and we are trying to stop people being rigid in their approaches to life. A quote we both like, is when I said about the guy who stood in front of the tank in Tiananmen Square, all the newspaper journalists and television guys say, 'Hey get me the guy who stood in front of the tank'. And my first reaction is, 'Get me the guy who's in the tank', and Max's is, 'The guy who's in the tank's girlfriend as well'. Drama is about looking at the complexities of these things, and sometimes journalism is about reducing something to a single sound-bite, or if there isn't a controversy actually creating one falsely. We don't go in with an agenda, we find what we find when we get there and we're constantly surprised, and we want our audiences to be surprised as well.

KEEPING IT REAL

Documentary Theatre

In 1976, Max Stafford-Clark and William Gaskill's Joint Stock Theatre Group produced *Yesterday's News*. As Gaskill tells it, they were at a loss for what play to do next, and decided to look through the newspapers for a story. The play was written from the company's subsequent interviews with Angolan mercenaries.

Stafford-Clark used the technique in 1983 at the Royal Court. *Falkland Sound* gave voice to many people touched by the conflict: a woman who ran a support group for sailors' wives in Plymouth; a journalist who'd been embedded with the invading forces on the ship The Canberra. A shell-shocked Scots Guard talked to the actors, as did a teacher from the Islands, and an Argentinan woman resident in London who listened in horror to the rolling news of the war.

Out of Joint's first verbatim project, *A State Affair* (Robin Soans 2000), was a companion piece to a revival of *Rita, Sue and Bob Too* by the late Andrea Dunbar. Her seminal play was first performed at the Court in 1982, since when the Bradford housing estate on which Dunbar had lived suffered a deeply destructive heroin and crime epidemic. Max Stafford-Clark says:

> *I knew that heroin had become a major problem on these estates. What I hadn't expected was the drive and the commitment of the various care-workers we spoke to: their non-judgmental approach and willingness to cope with young people as victims of social conditions. Whereas the newspapers have exhibited a readiness to blame and to find scapegoats.*

This is verbatim theatre's great strength – an advantage it perhaps has over its cousin, investigative journalism. It looks at the whole picture, a wide range of view-points, without needing to find a specific 'angle'. Although of course, the author of a verbatim play edits, censors, and rearranges at will, just as the editor of a documentary would. David Hare acknowledges that the apparent neutrality of the art-form is an illusion: of his play about British Rail's privatisation, *The Permanent Way*, he conceded, 'I'm all over it like a rash'. His more recent play *Stuff Happens* (about the build up to the Iraq War) openly combined verbatim dialogue with fictional, speculative scenes.

As well as discovering stories untold elsewhere, theatre turns an ongoing, messy event into a comprehensible overview. It brings the strands together, helping its audience evaluate events that may be too big, too close, too current. The Tricycle Theatre's *Justifying War* condensed the Hutton Inquiry into two hours of theatre. *Der Spiegel* commissioned Klaus Pohl's *Waiting Room Germany* to test the mood of Germany after reunification – its stories of gain and loss were told verbatim to the audience. *The Laramie Project* was less about the horrific abduction and murder of gay student Matthew Shepard than it was about the town's reactions to it – and to the media's depiction of them as red-necked white trash. And also from the US, *The Exonerated* depicted six innocent survivors on death row. Verbatim theatre can bring the key themes, as well as the specific details, into focus.

And verbatim theatre provides a new challenge for actors, because they are playing real people – people who may even be in the audience. The actors in Out of Joint's *Talking to Terrorists* and *The Permanent Way* did not attempt precisely to mimic their real-life counterparts (they did speak of their loyalty to them, the compulsion to 'do right' by them). Alecky Blythe's Recorded Delivery company takes this further. For example, her show *Come Out Eli*, based around the Hackney siege of December 2002 was performed by actors listening, through earpieces, to recordings of the people they were presenting. While the audience were asked to accept the convention of the same actor playing an asian man, a young black woman and a white middle-class housewife, they knew that every word, and every 'um' and 'er', were authentic. Her latest is *The Girlfriend Experience*, for which Blythe spent time interviewing girls working in a brothel – a world few of us are likely to encounter first hand.

In the last few years, a new trend has emerged in presenting truth and authenticity in theatre, namely site-specific and promenade performances. Look Left Look Right's play *The Caravan* told the stories of those worst affected by the 2007 floods, and was indeed staged in its own temporary accommodation – a caravan parked outside the Royal Court Theatre and elsewhere. *The Container*, a play about illegal immigrants, is performed inside a shipping container. And the recent *Stovepipe*, a fictional and in many ways conventional play about mercenaries in post-invasion Iraq, was staged across a number of rooms and spaces in a disused shopping centre, kitted out as a bar, a hotel room, an arms trading fair and so on, perhaps to help the audience feel as disoriented as the characters.

These are all attempts at a kind of truth. Do verbatim texts and immersive surroundings make for a more truthful art? Perhaps or perhaps not – the best fictional writing has its own truths. But these are all attempts at connecting, and understanding, as fully as possible, with the added frisson that comes with discovering something of other people's lives.

Jon Bradfield